THE SEA FAIRIES

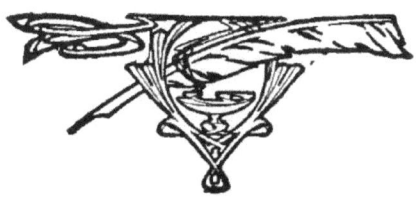

ILLUSTRATED BY
JOHN R. NEILL

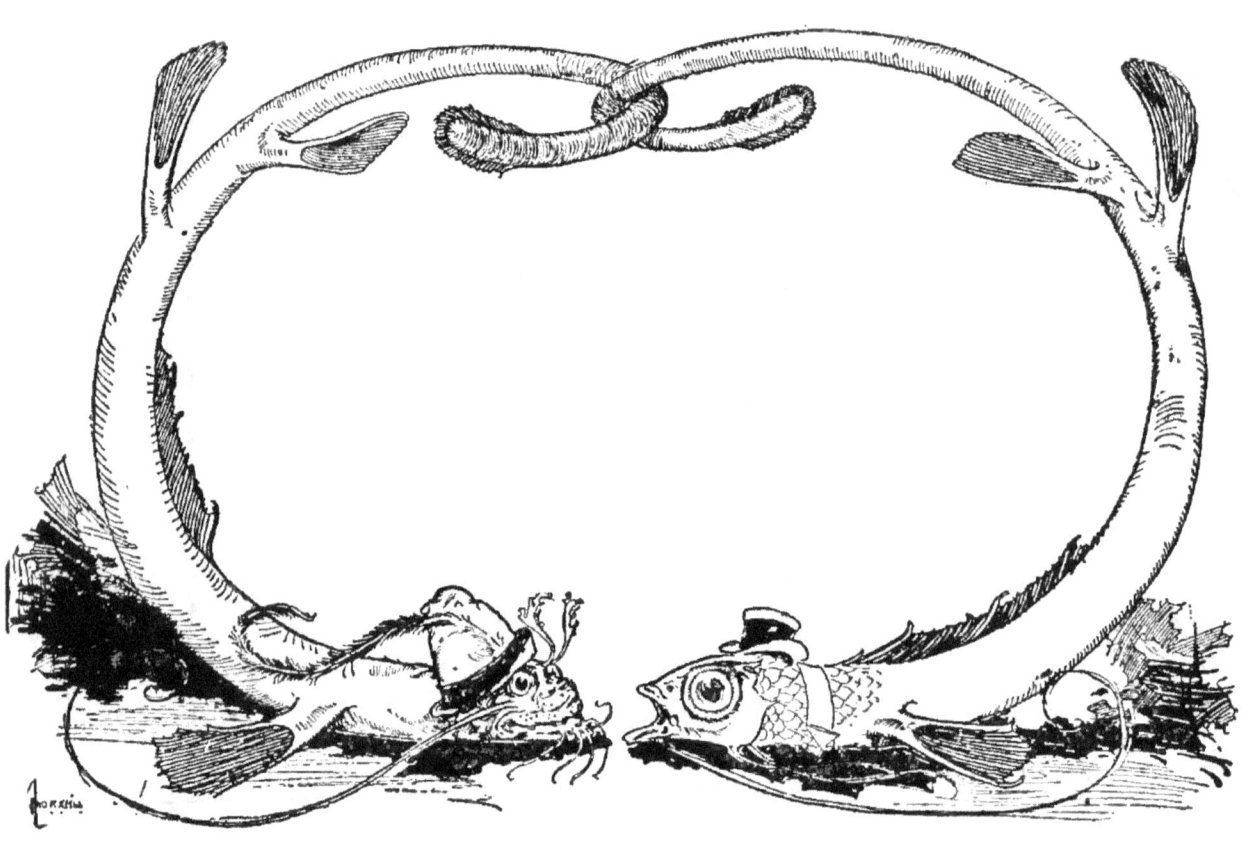

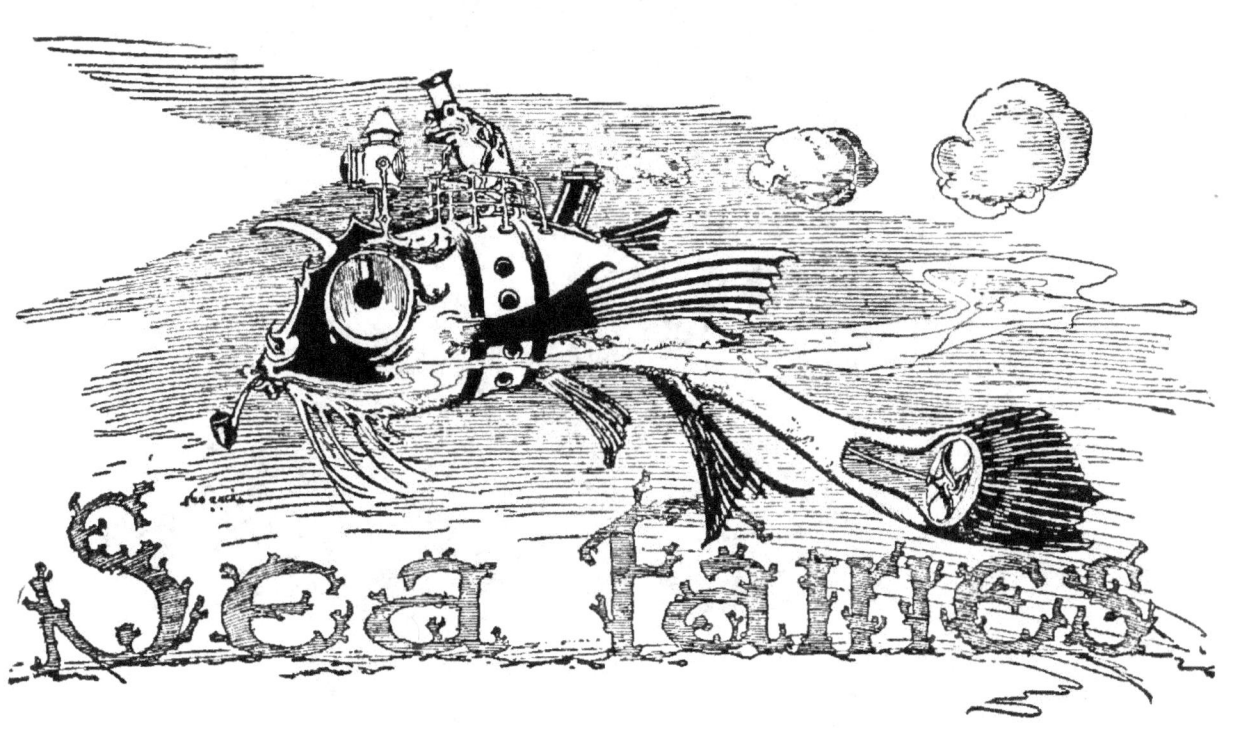

Sea fairies

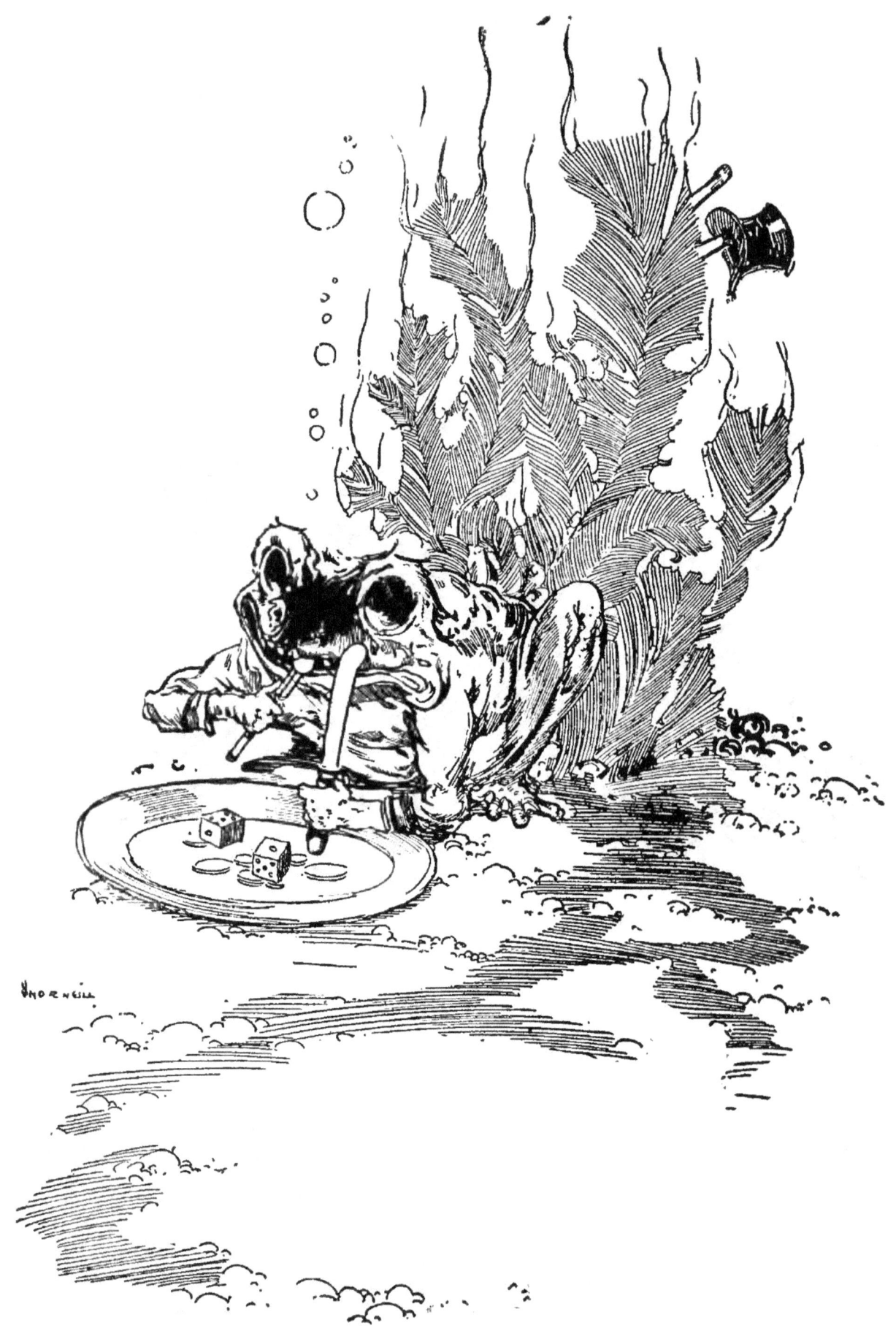

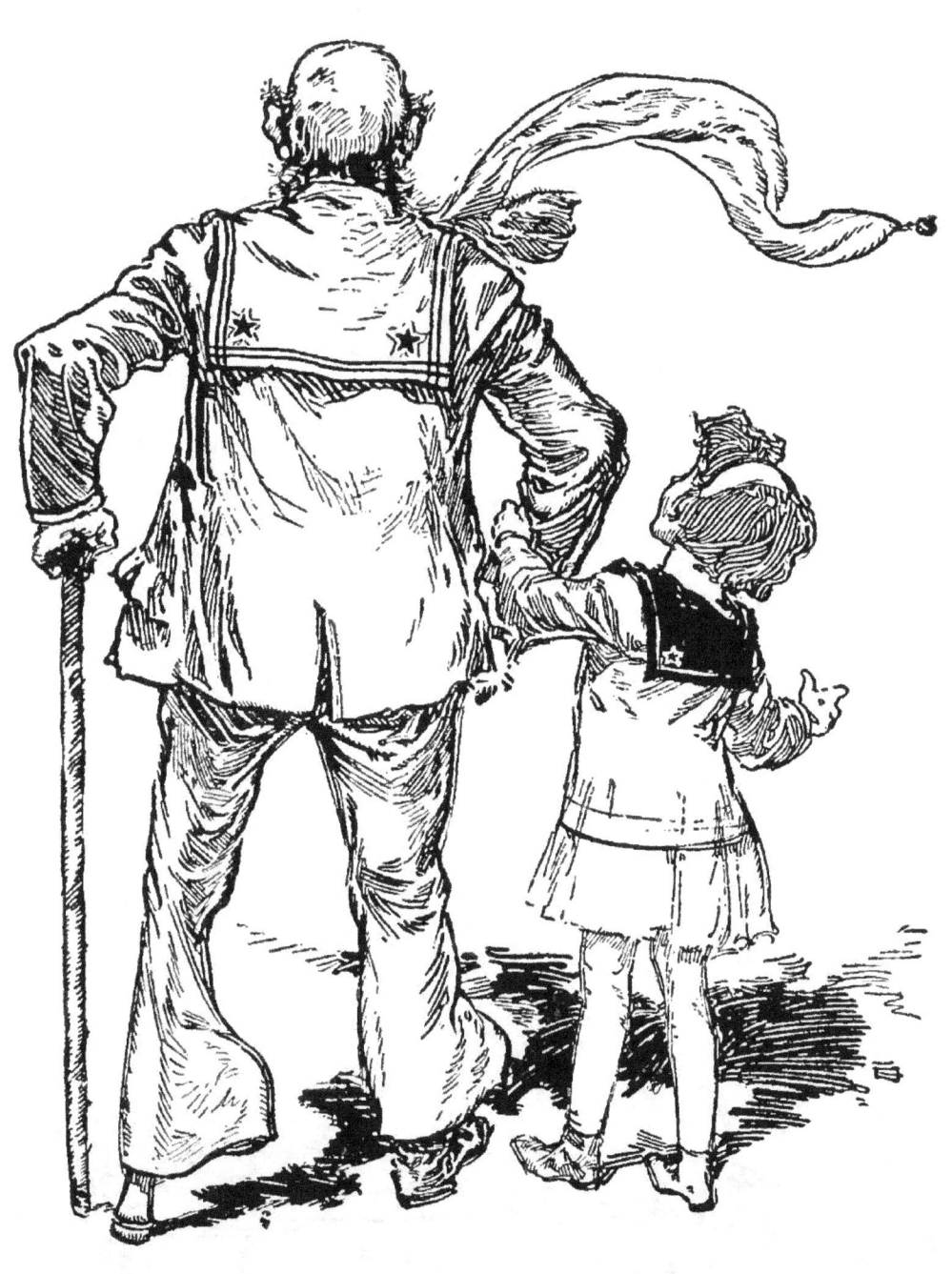

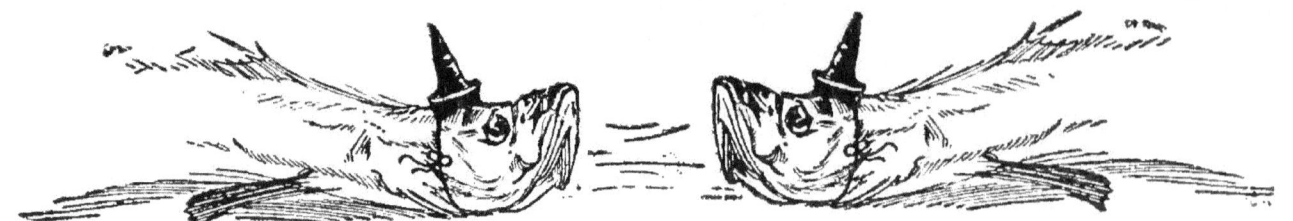

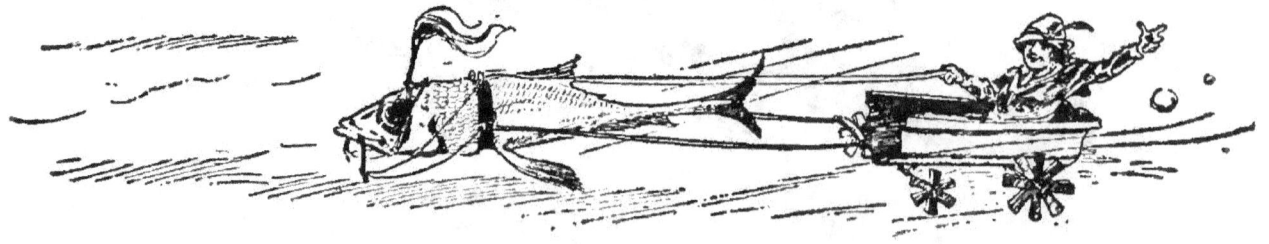

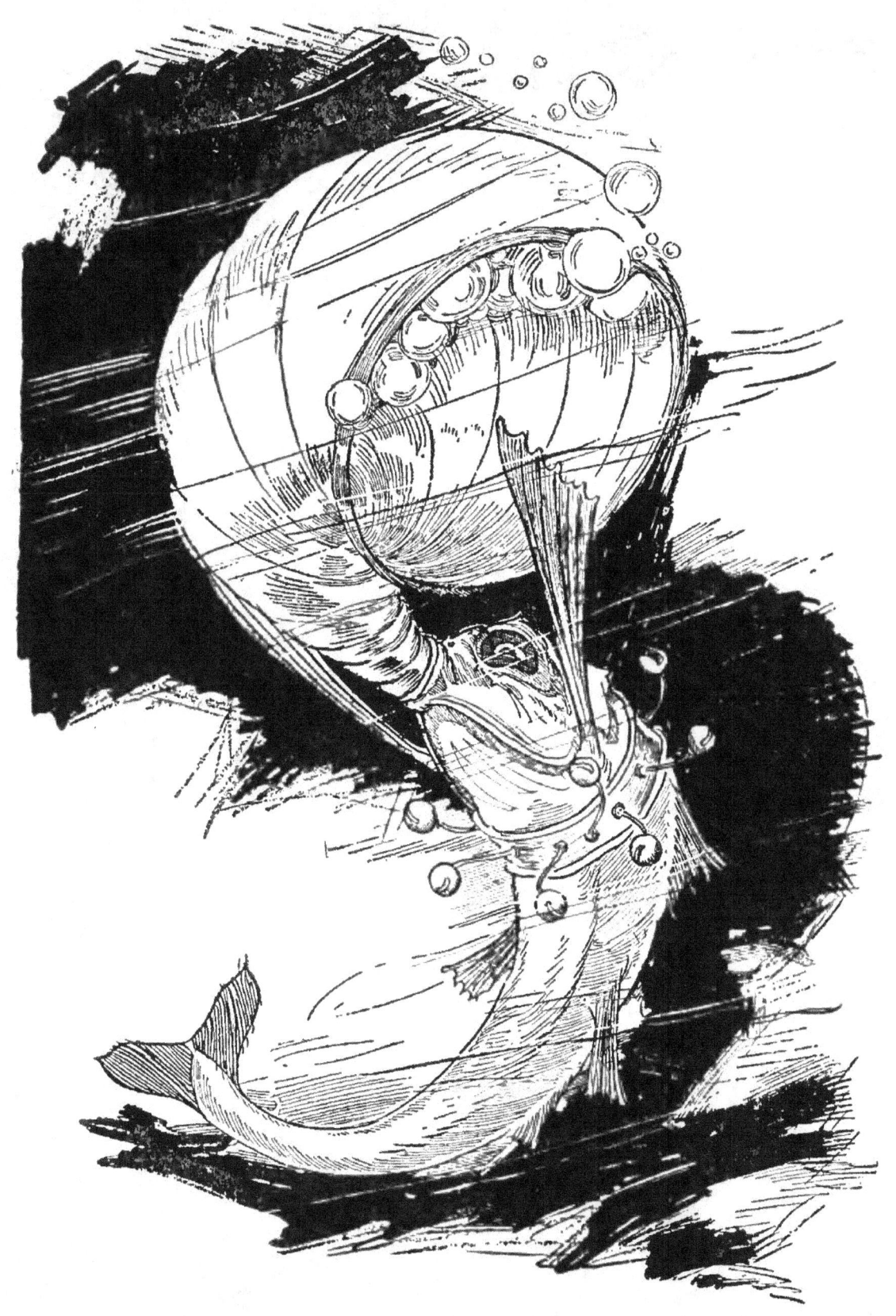

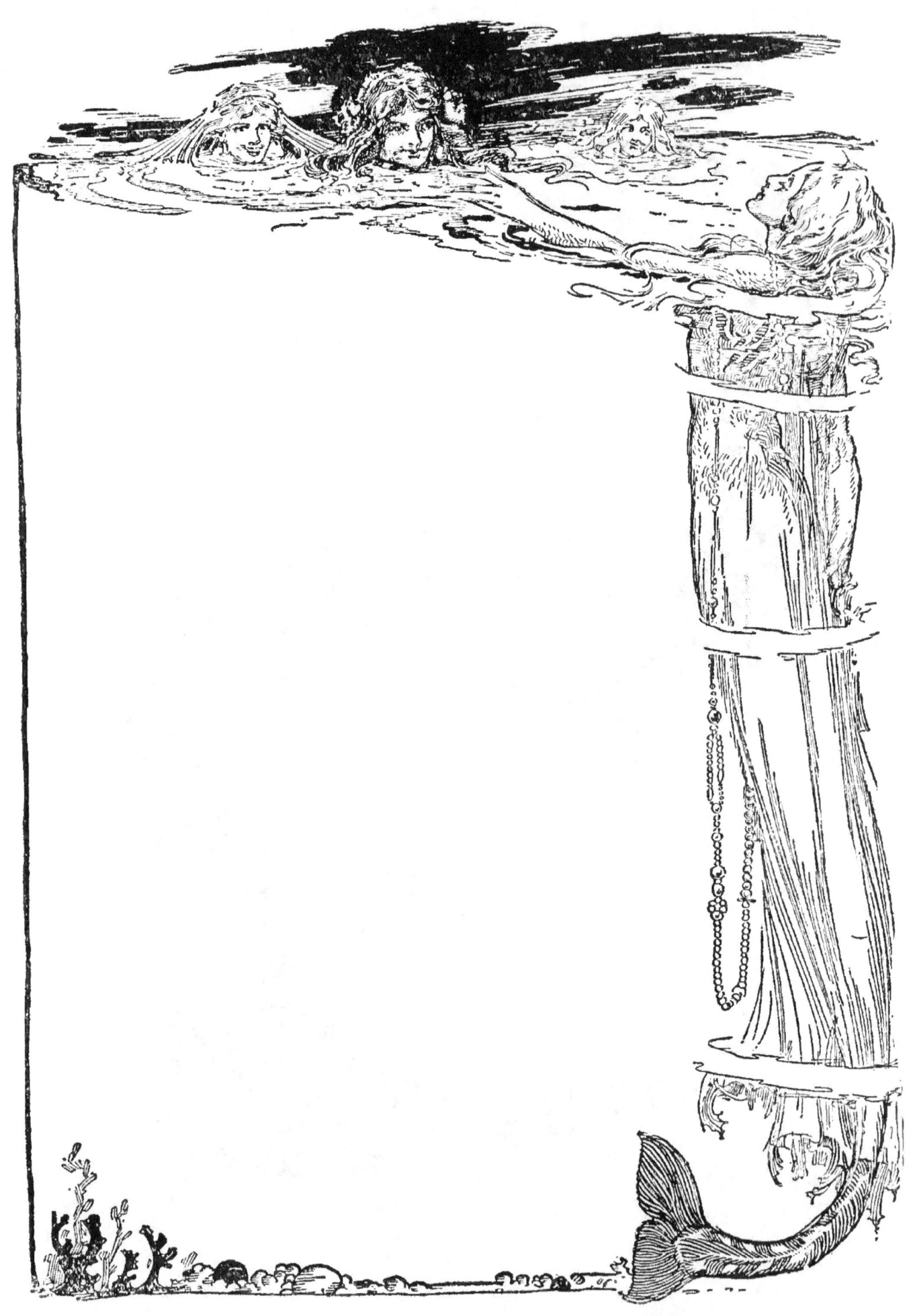

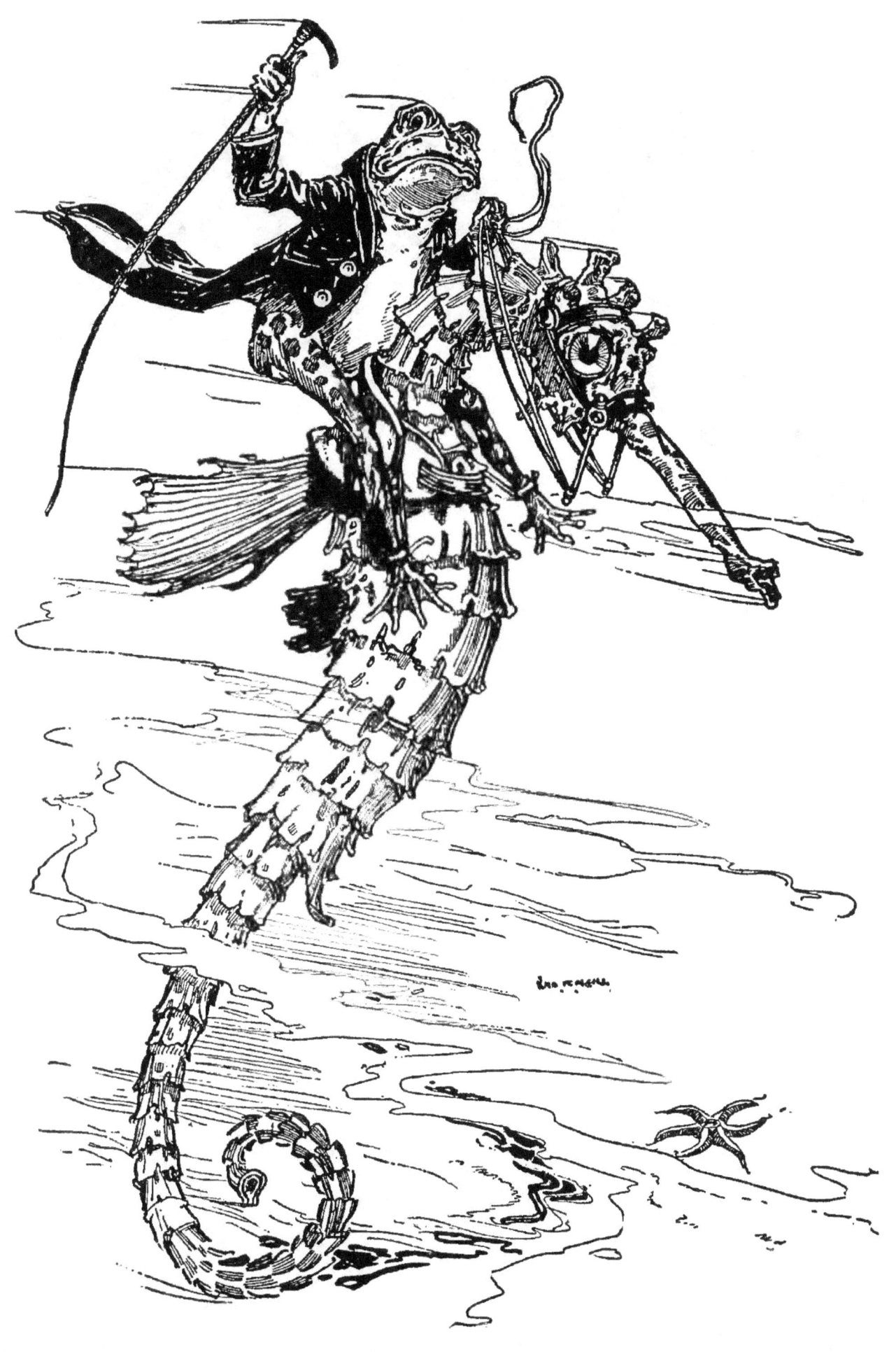

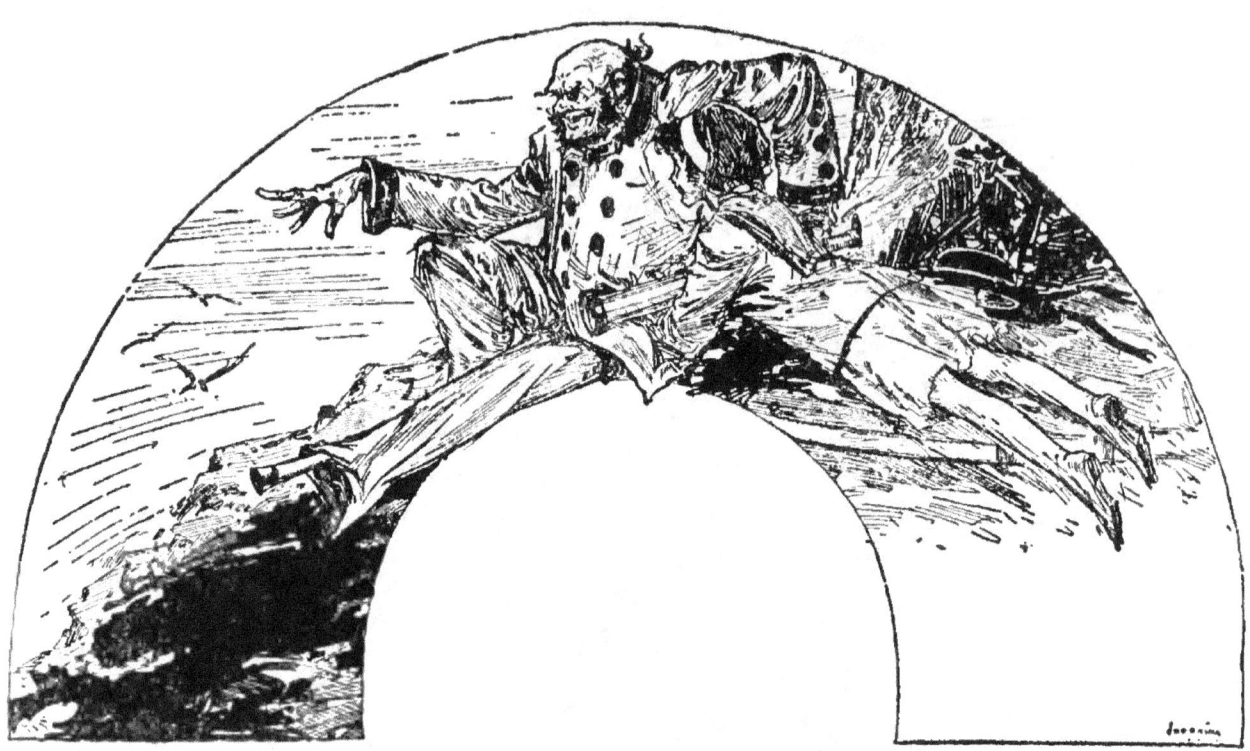

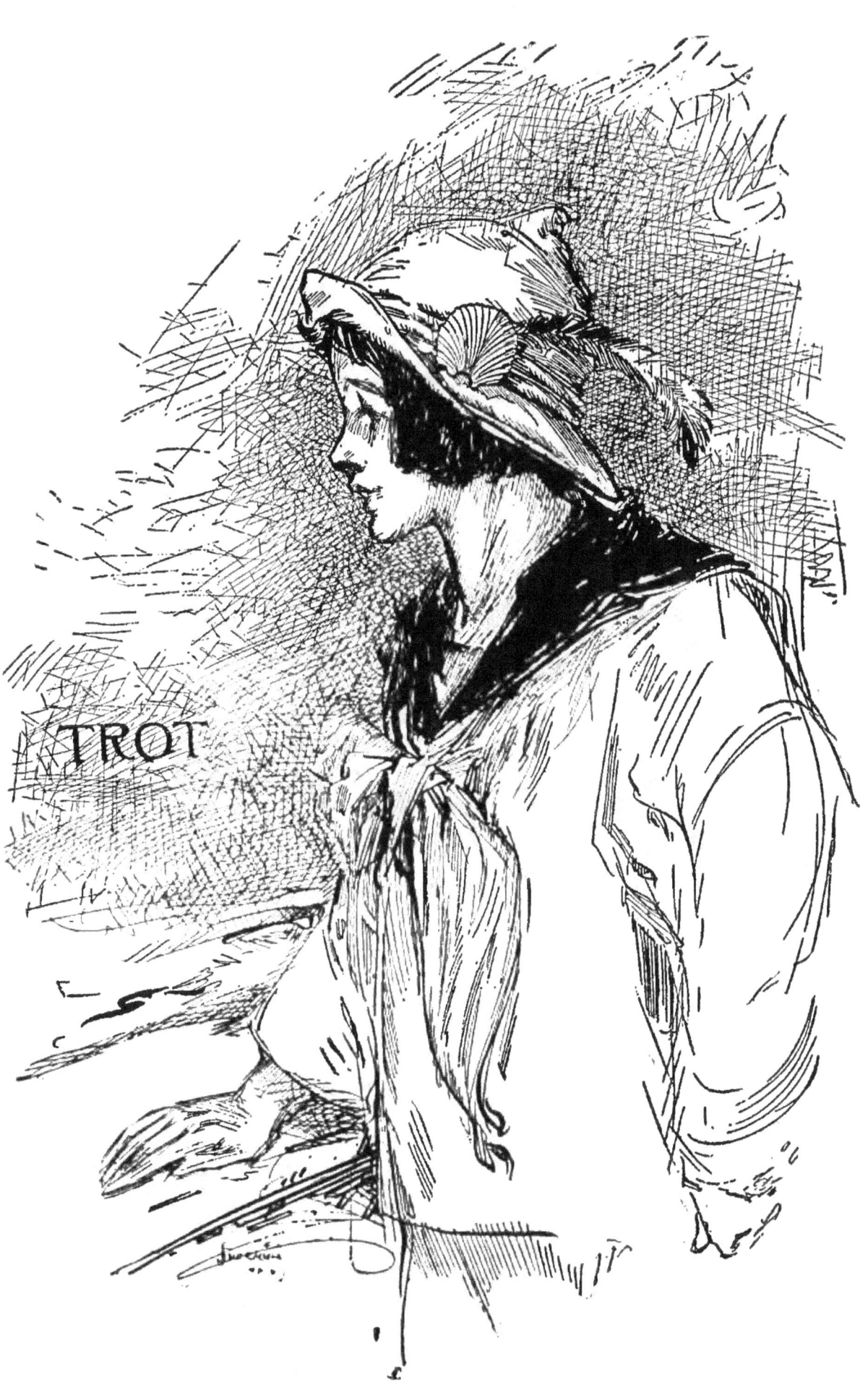

TROT

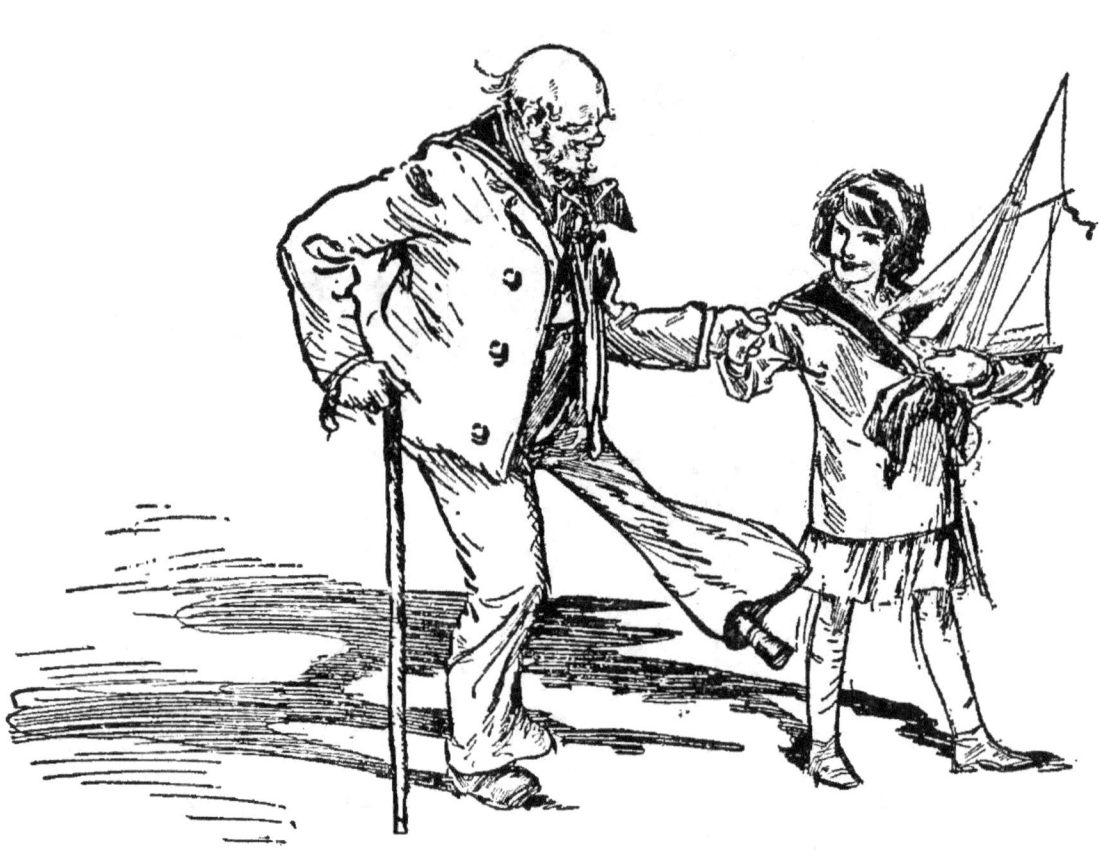

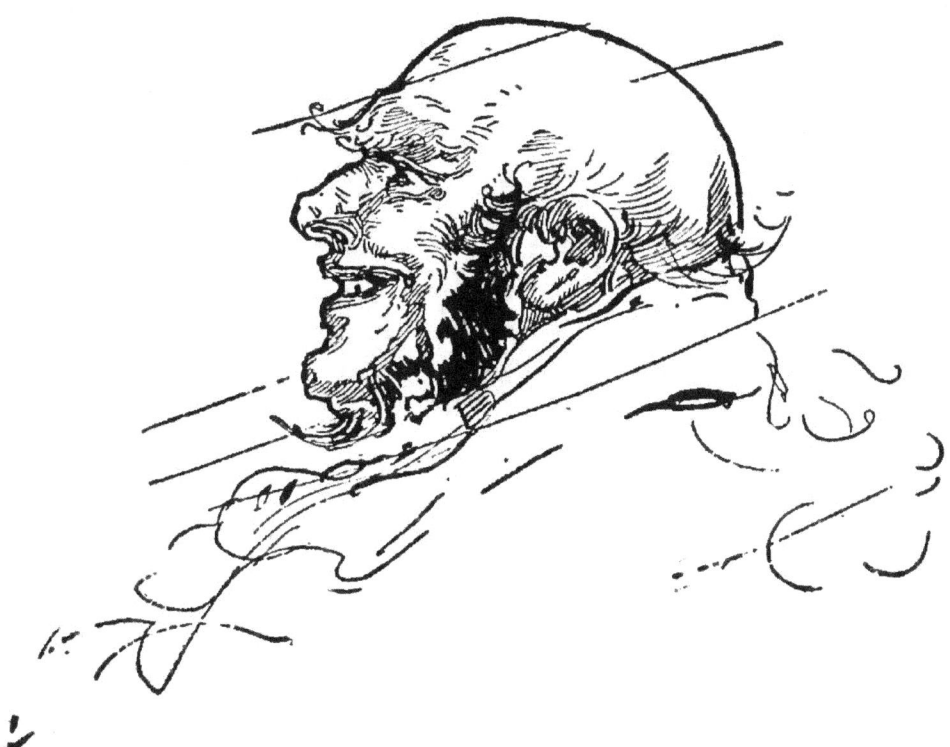

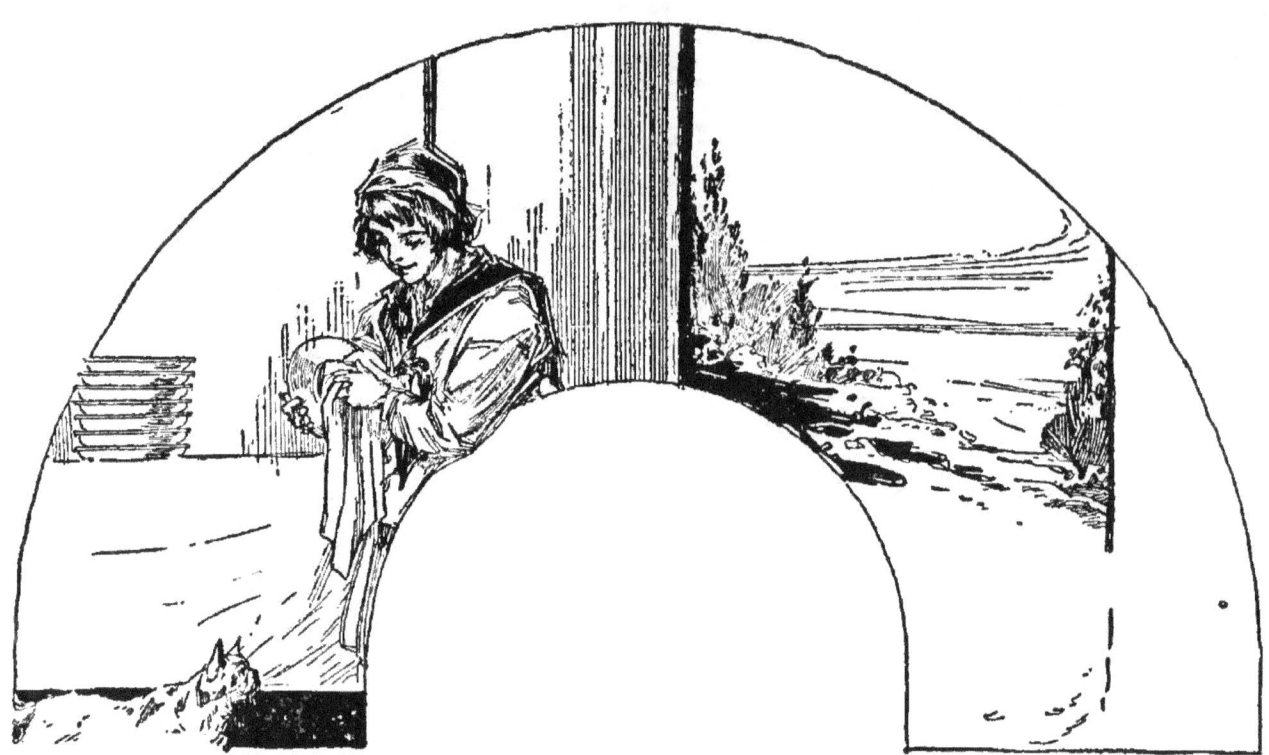

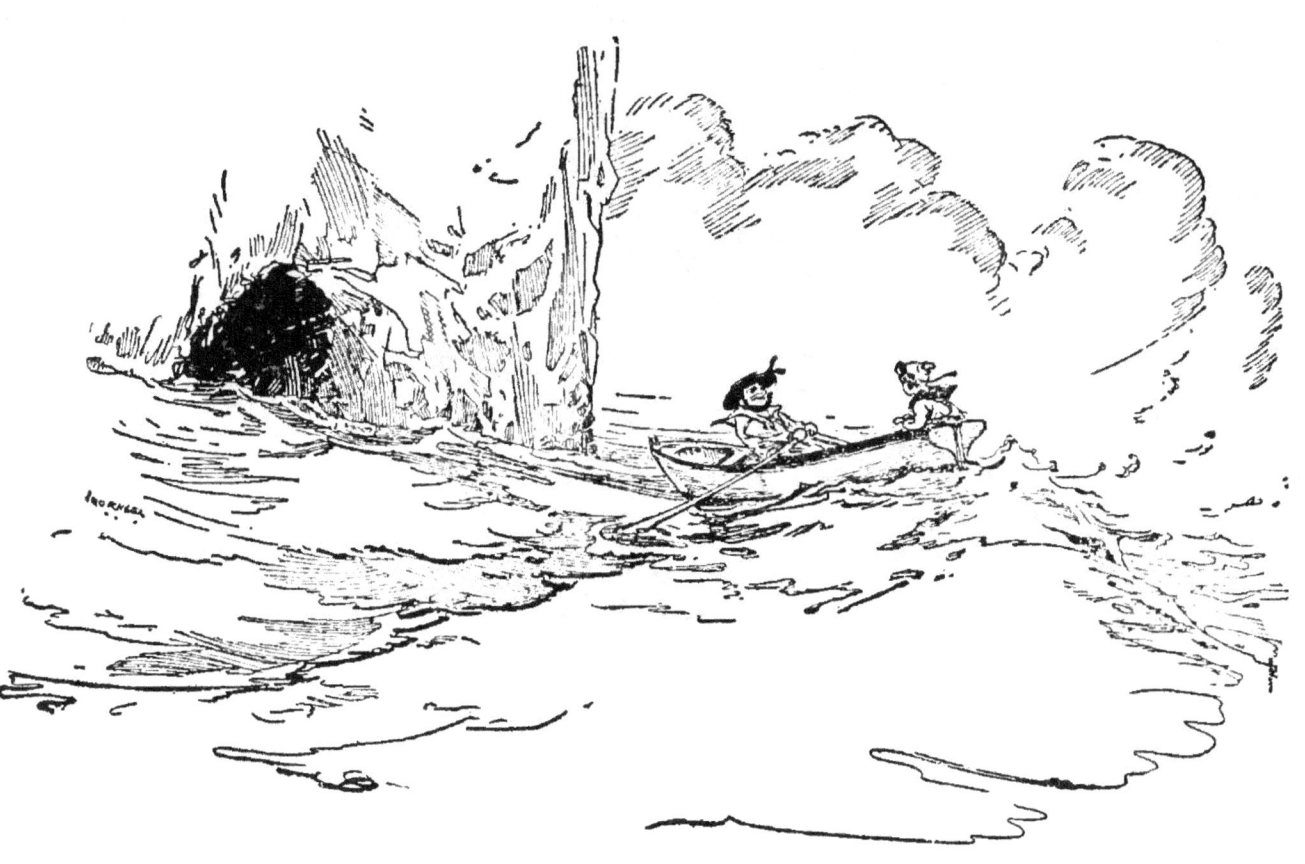

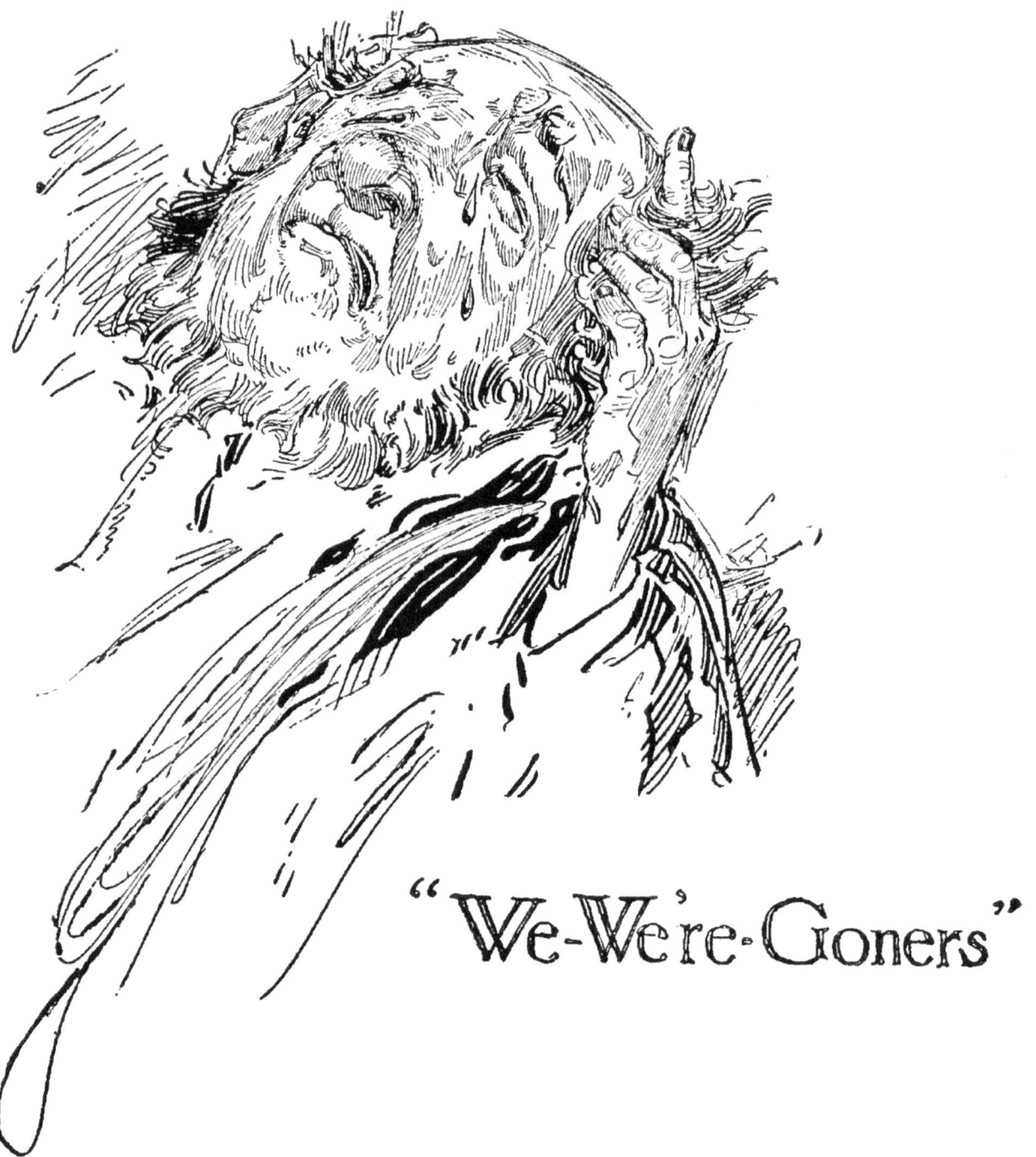

"We-We're-Goners"

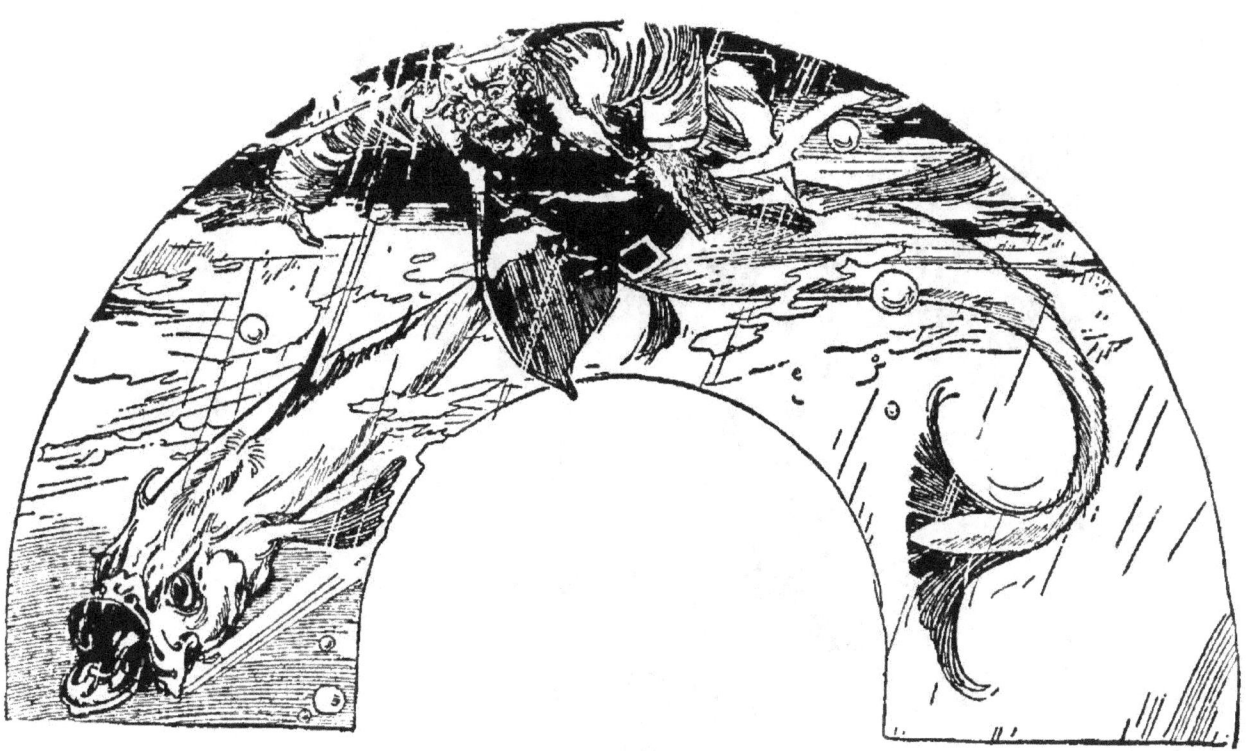

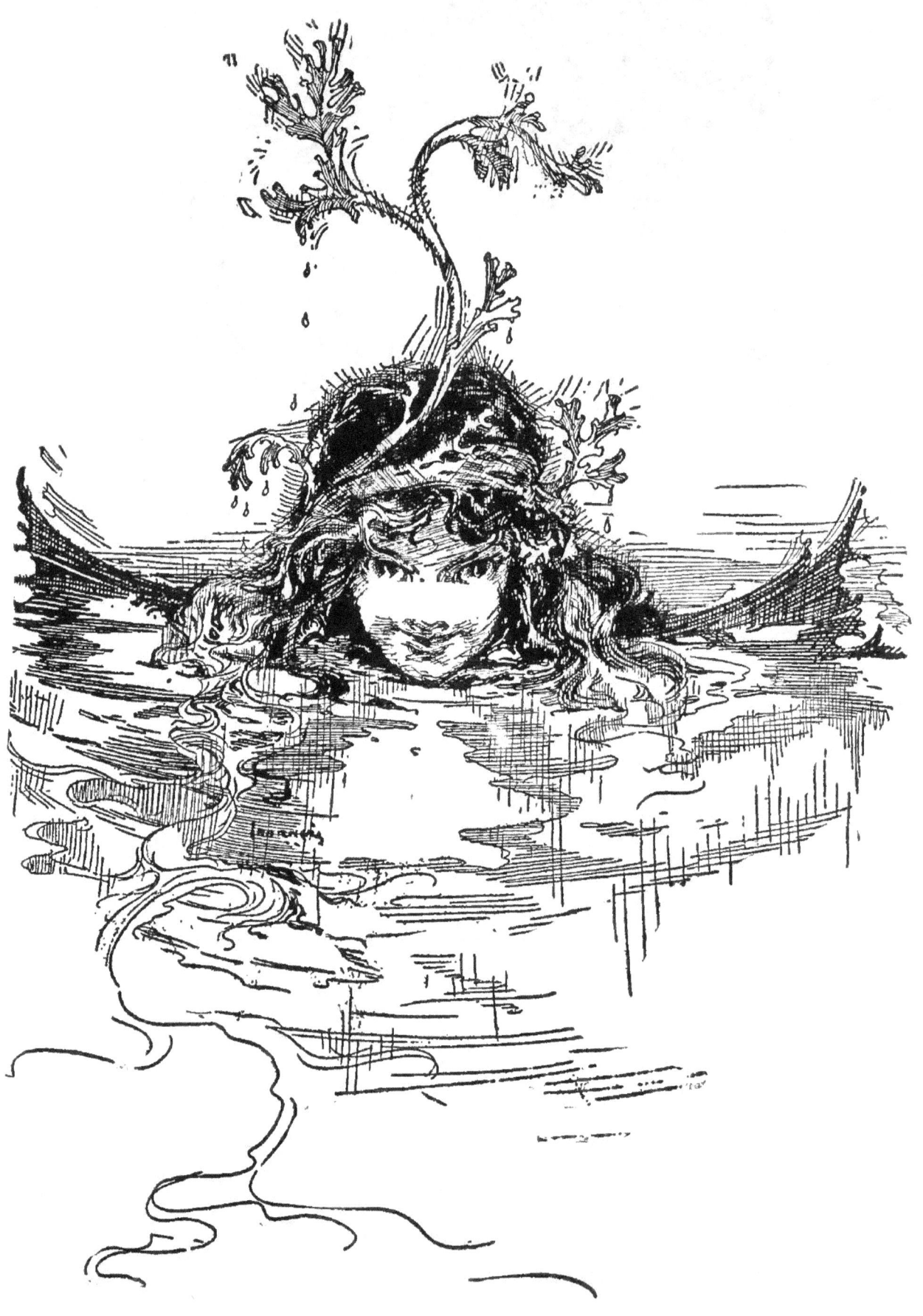

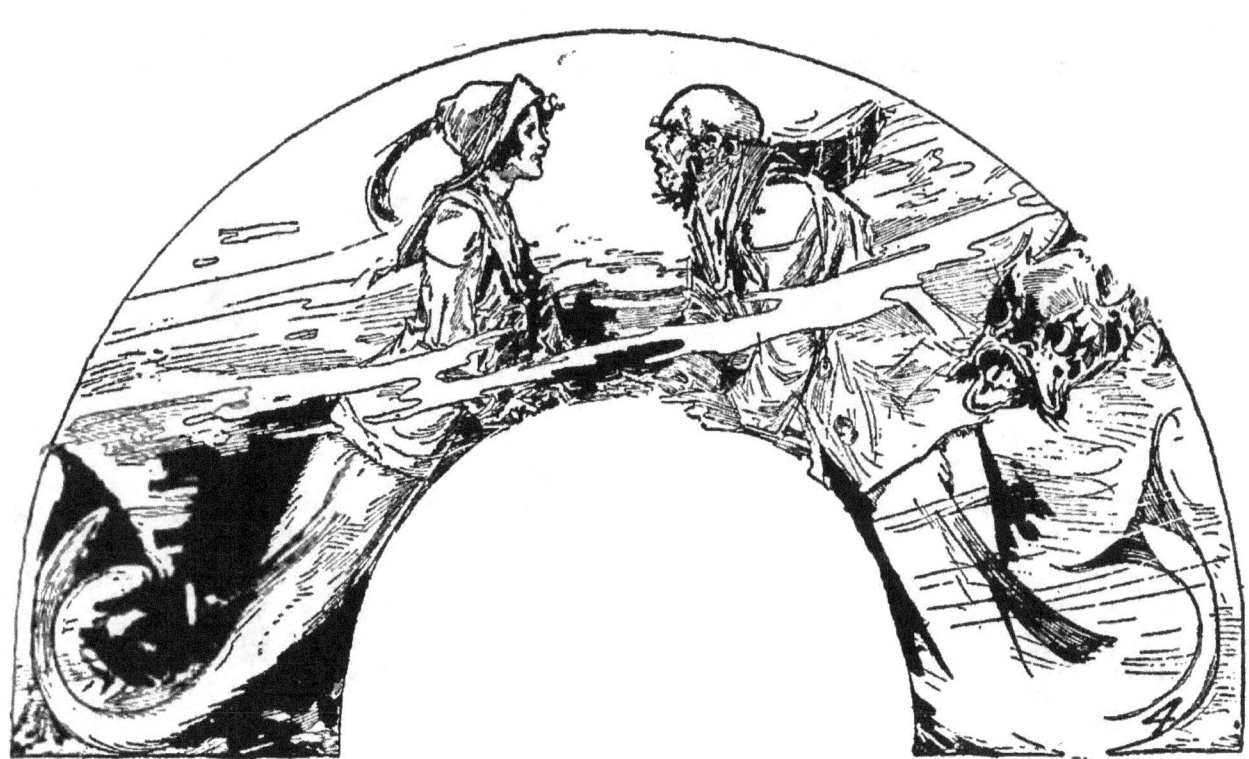

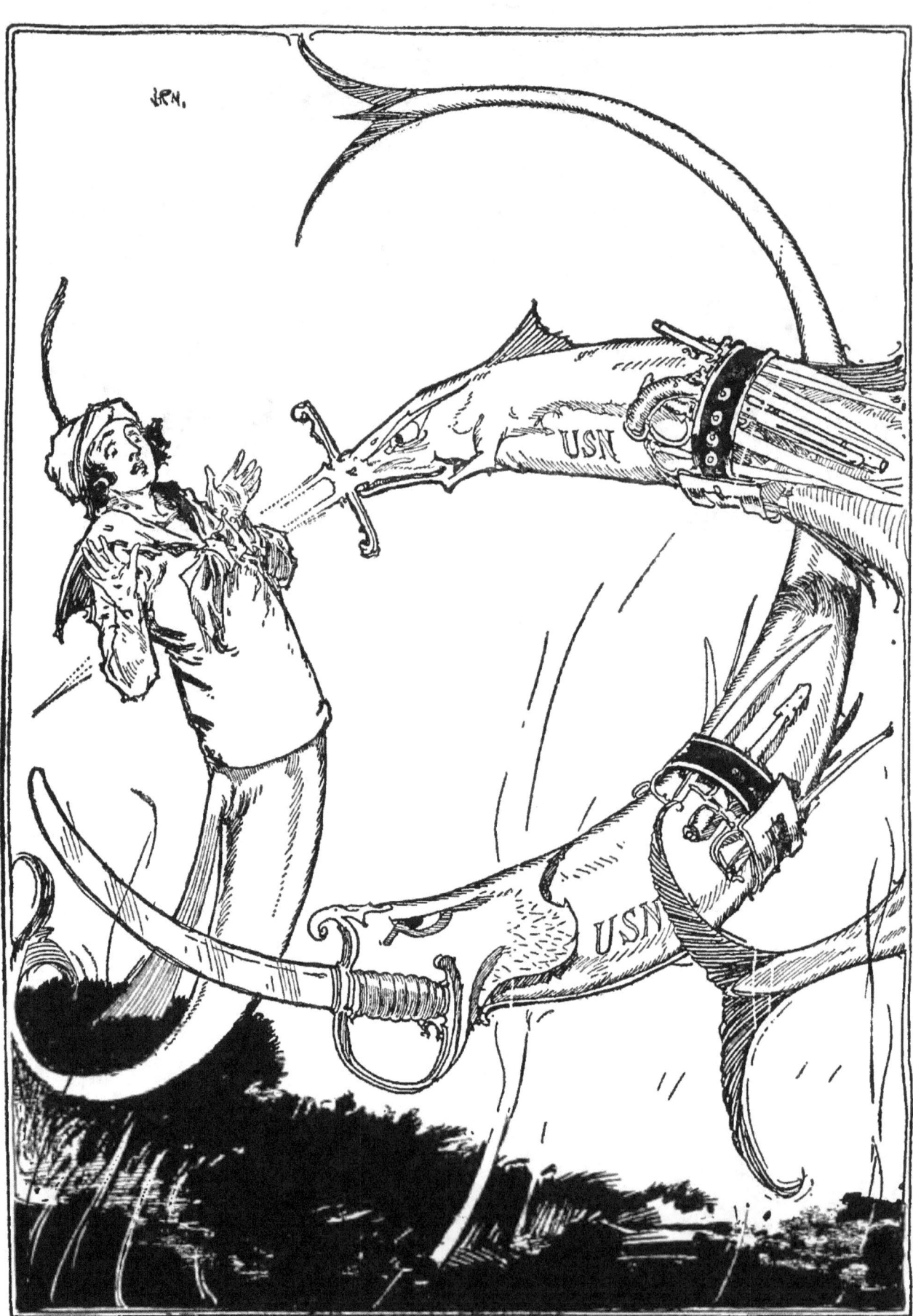

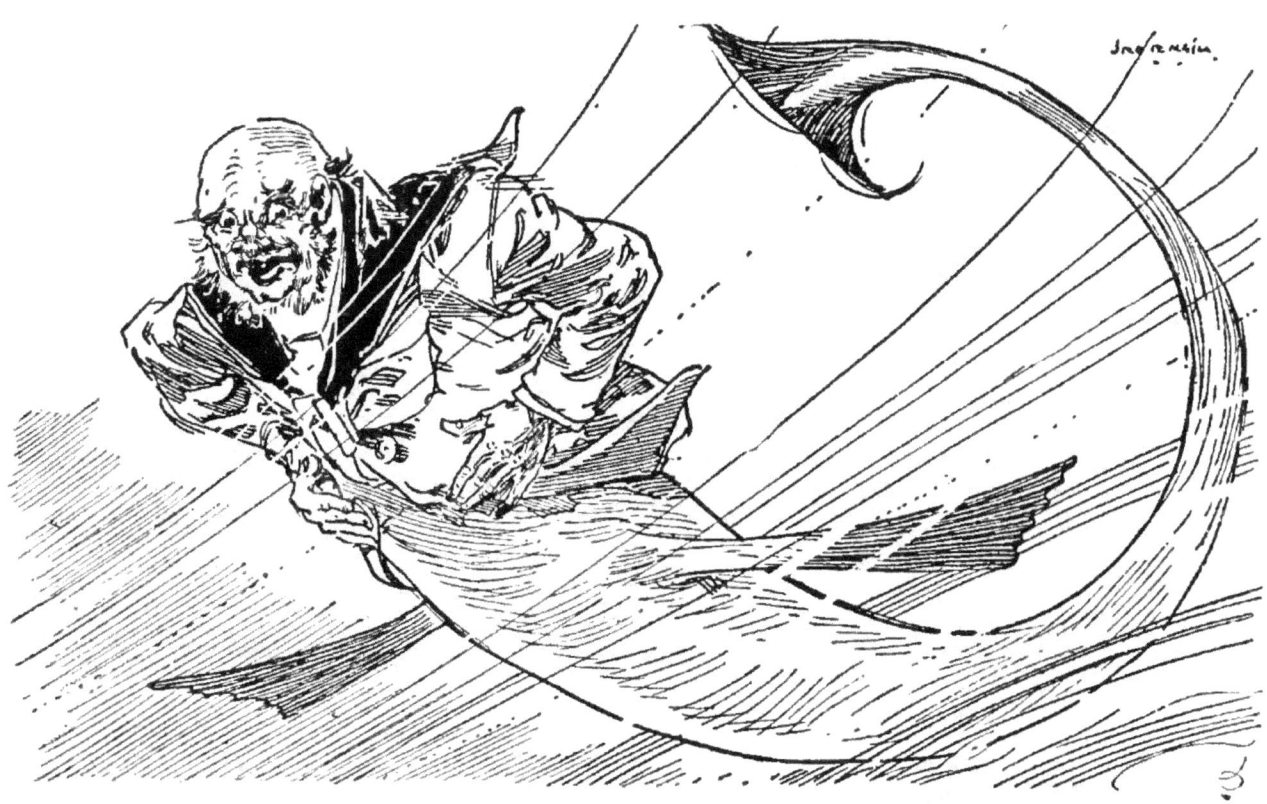

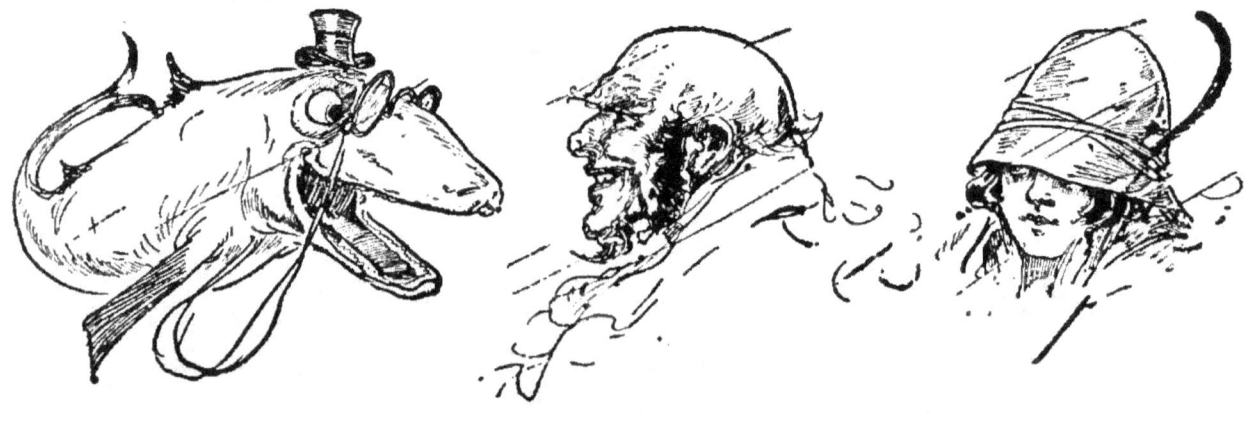

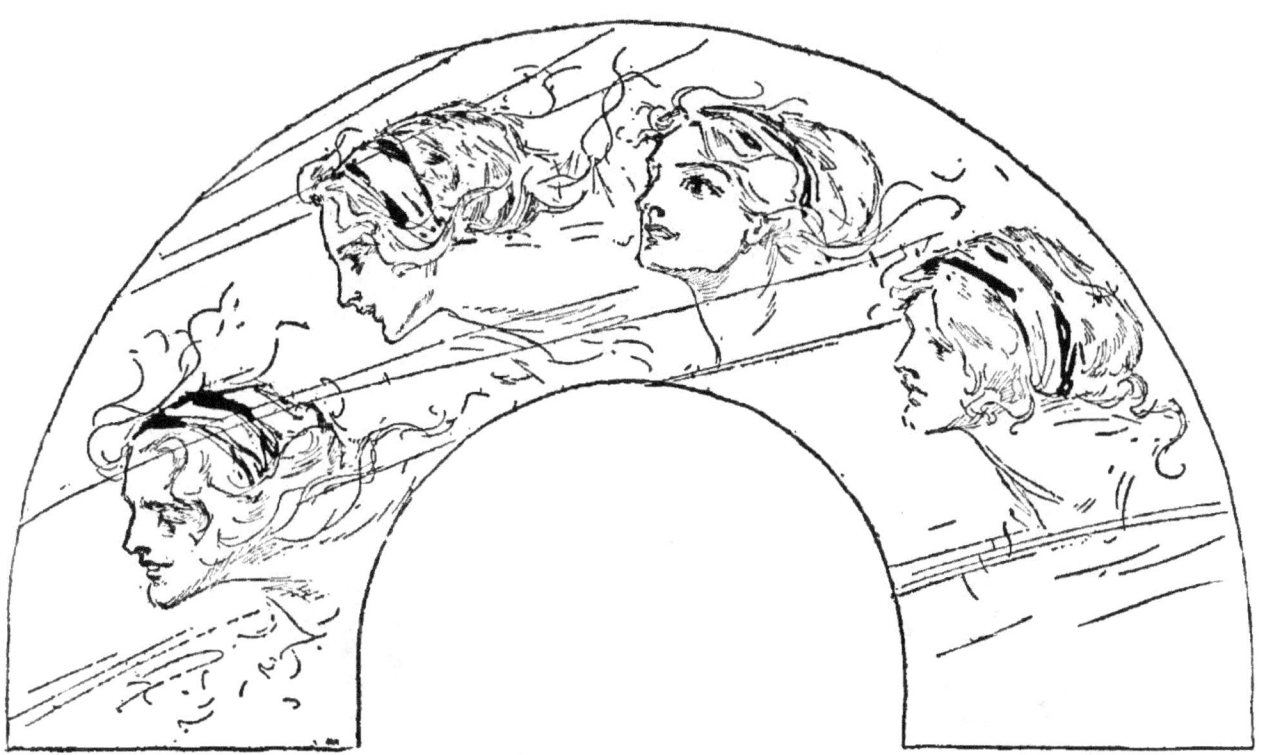

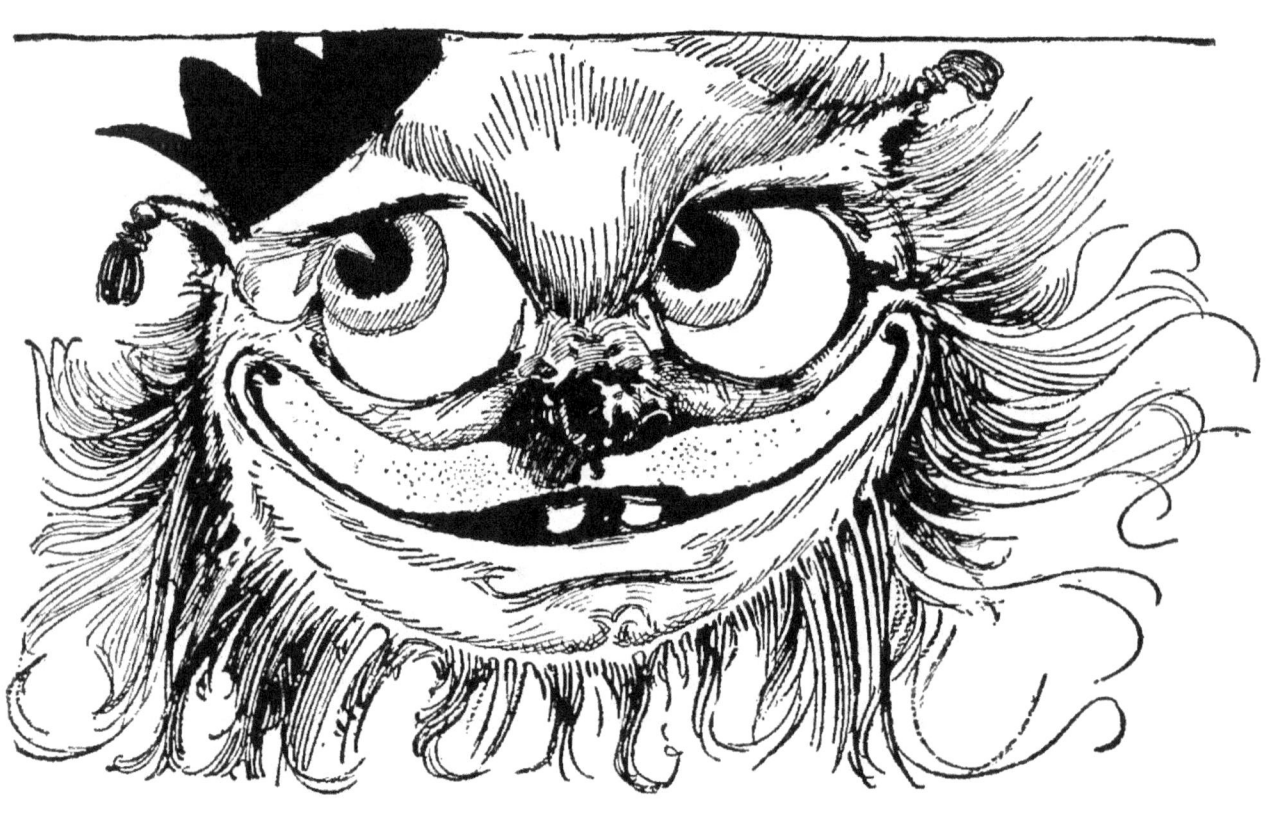

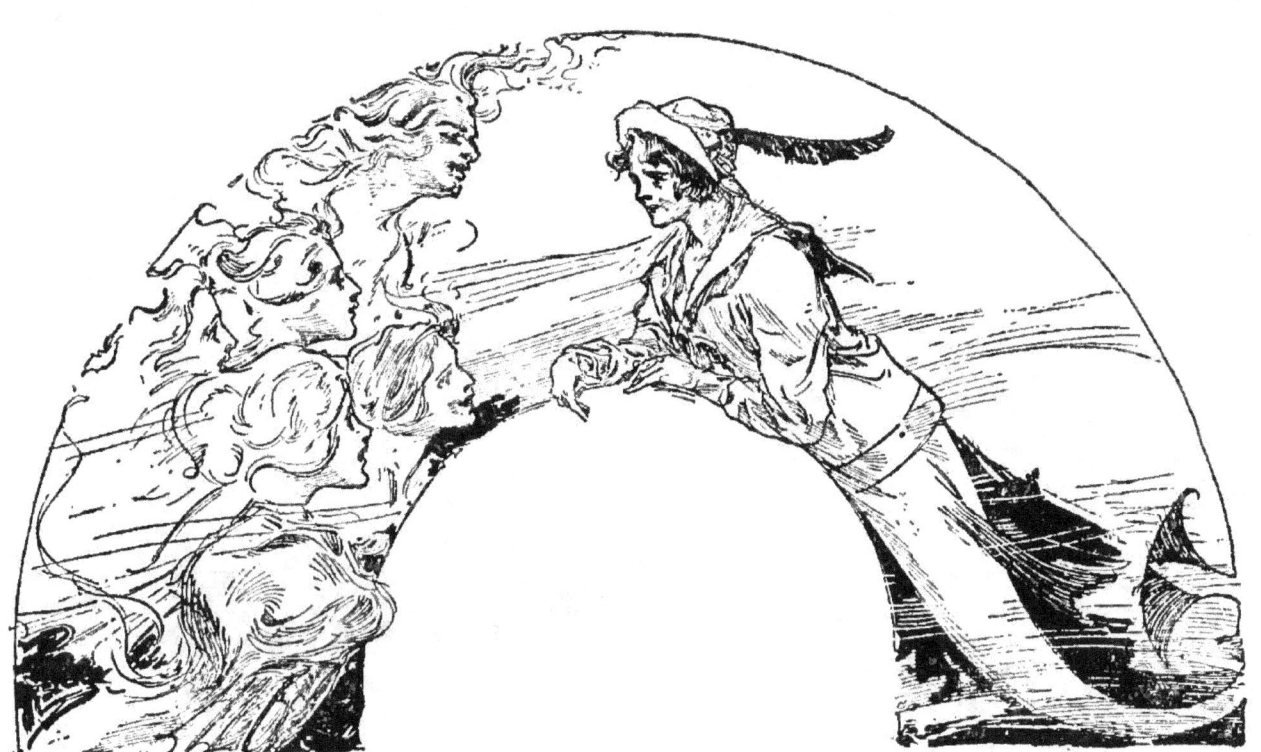

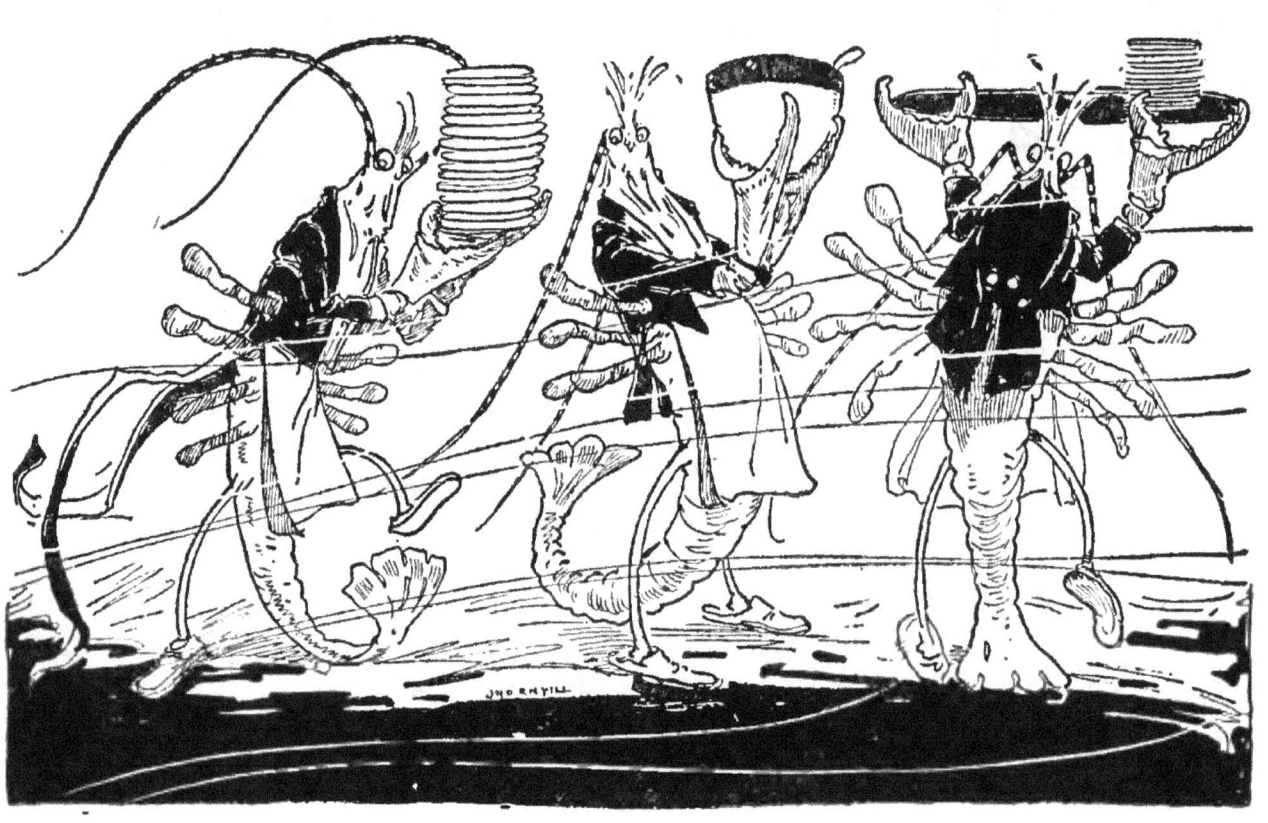

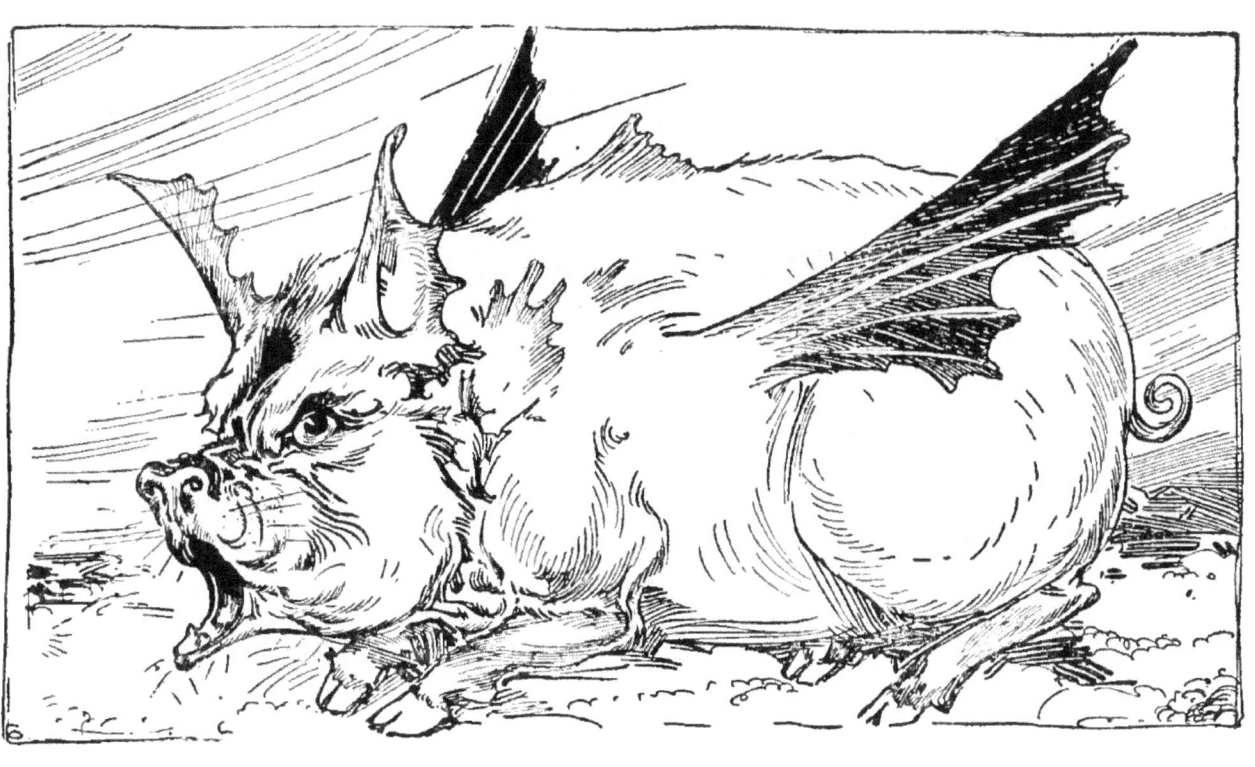

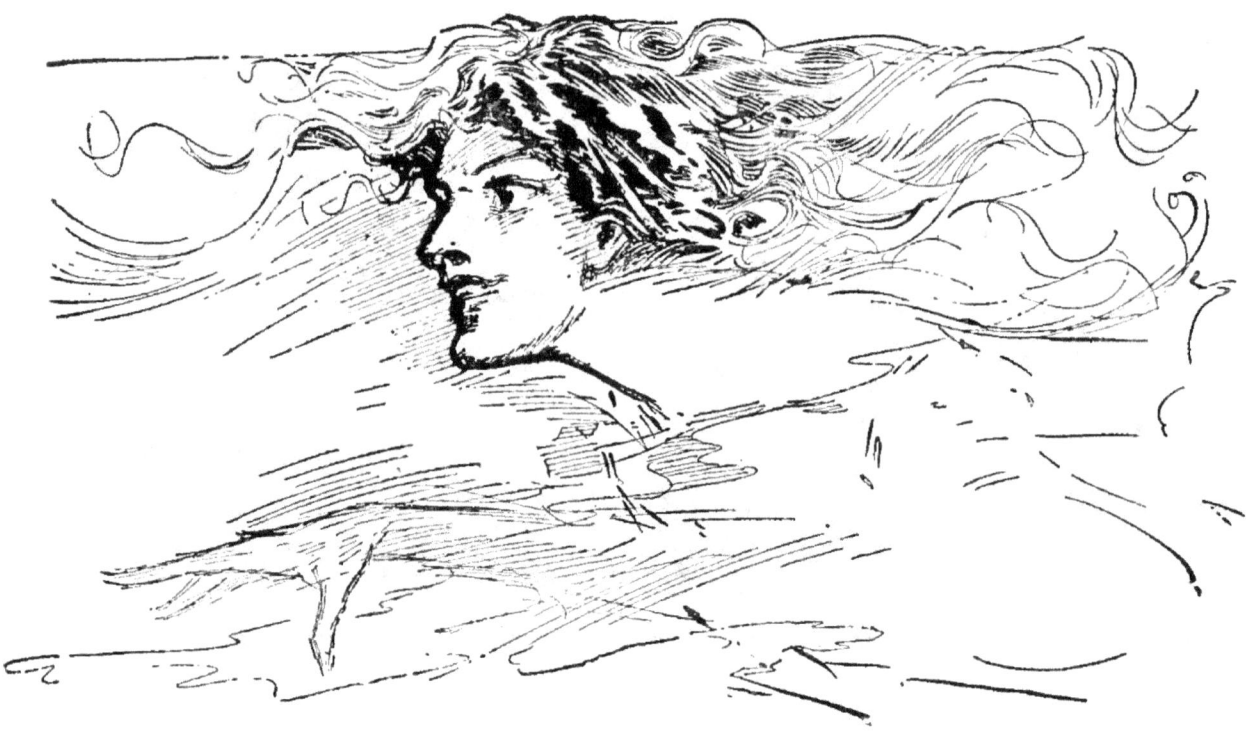

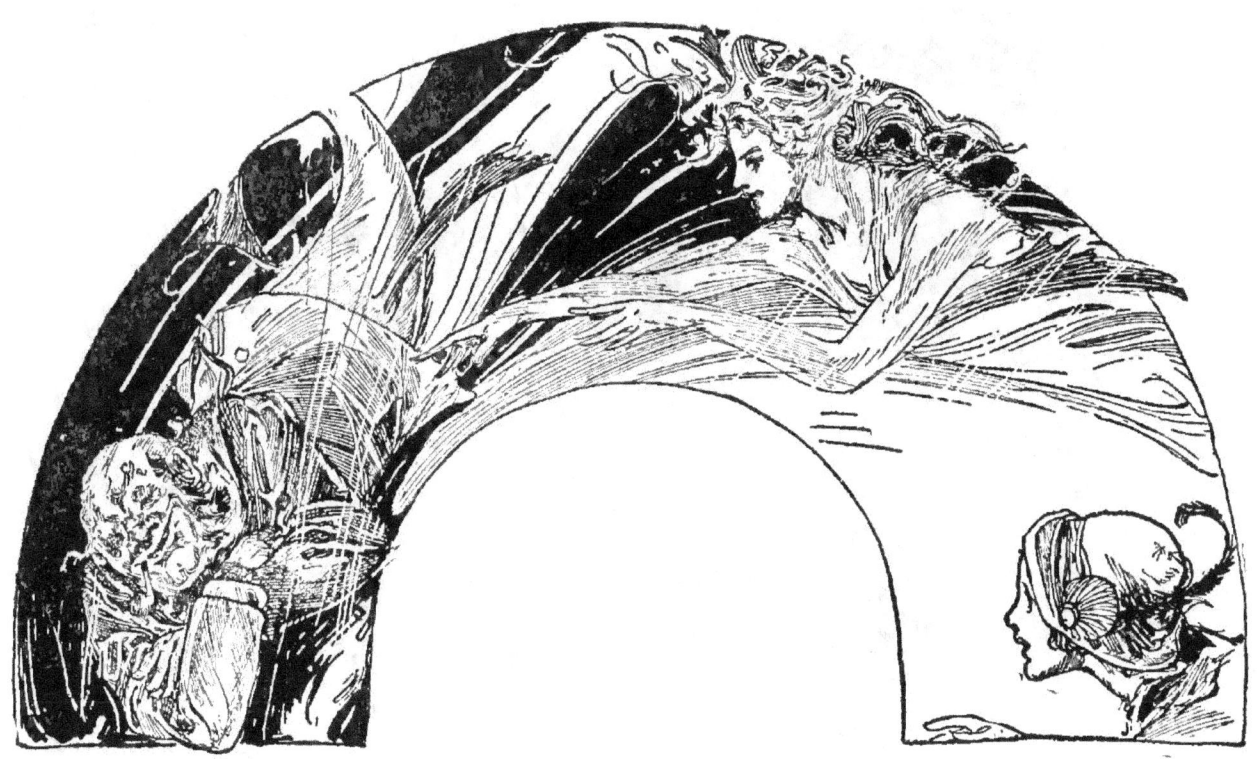

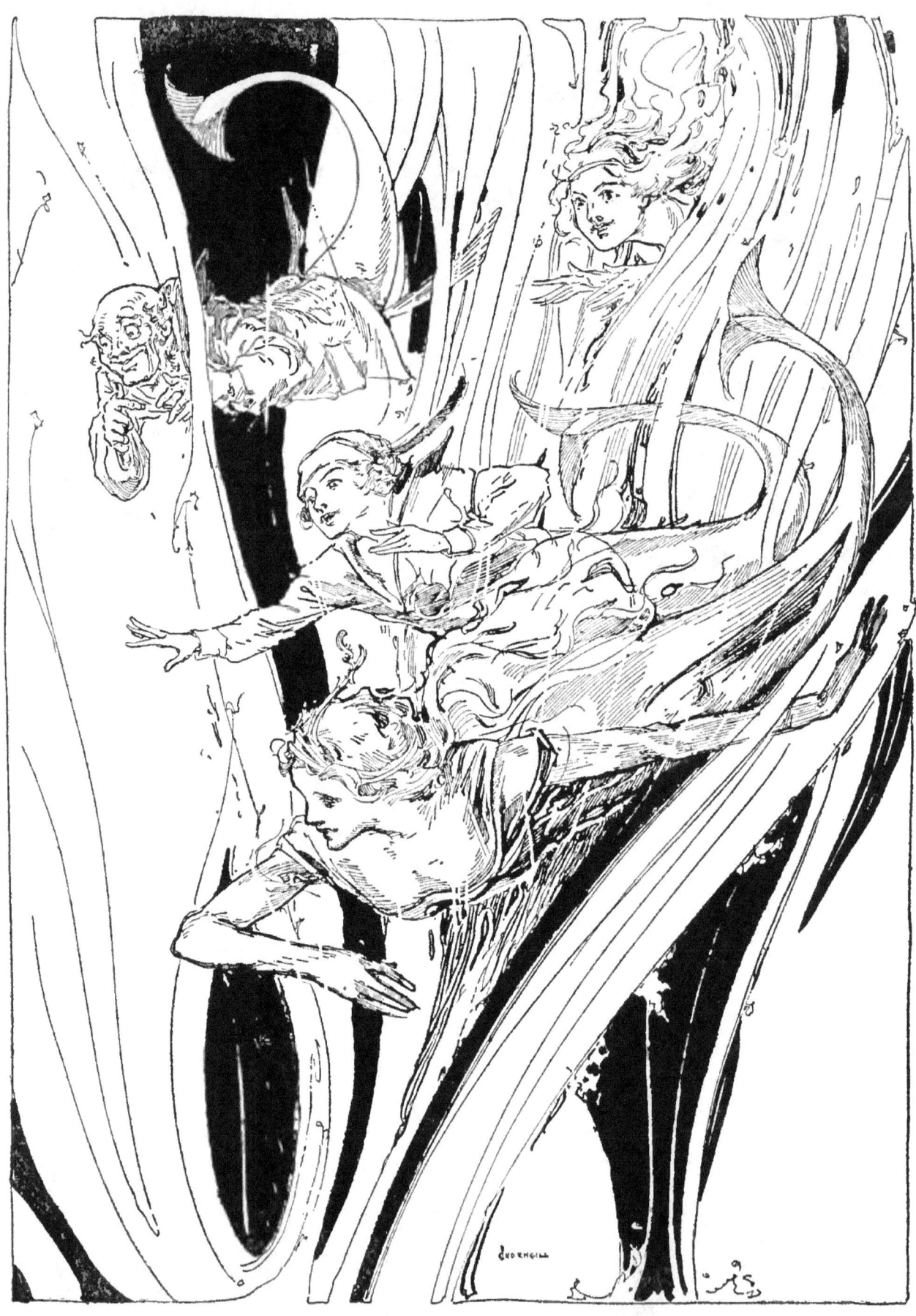

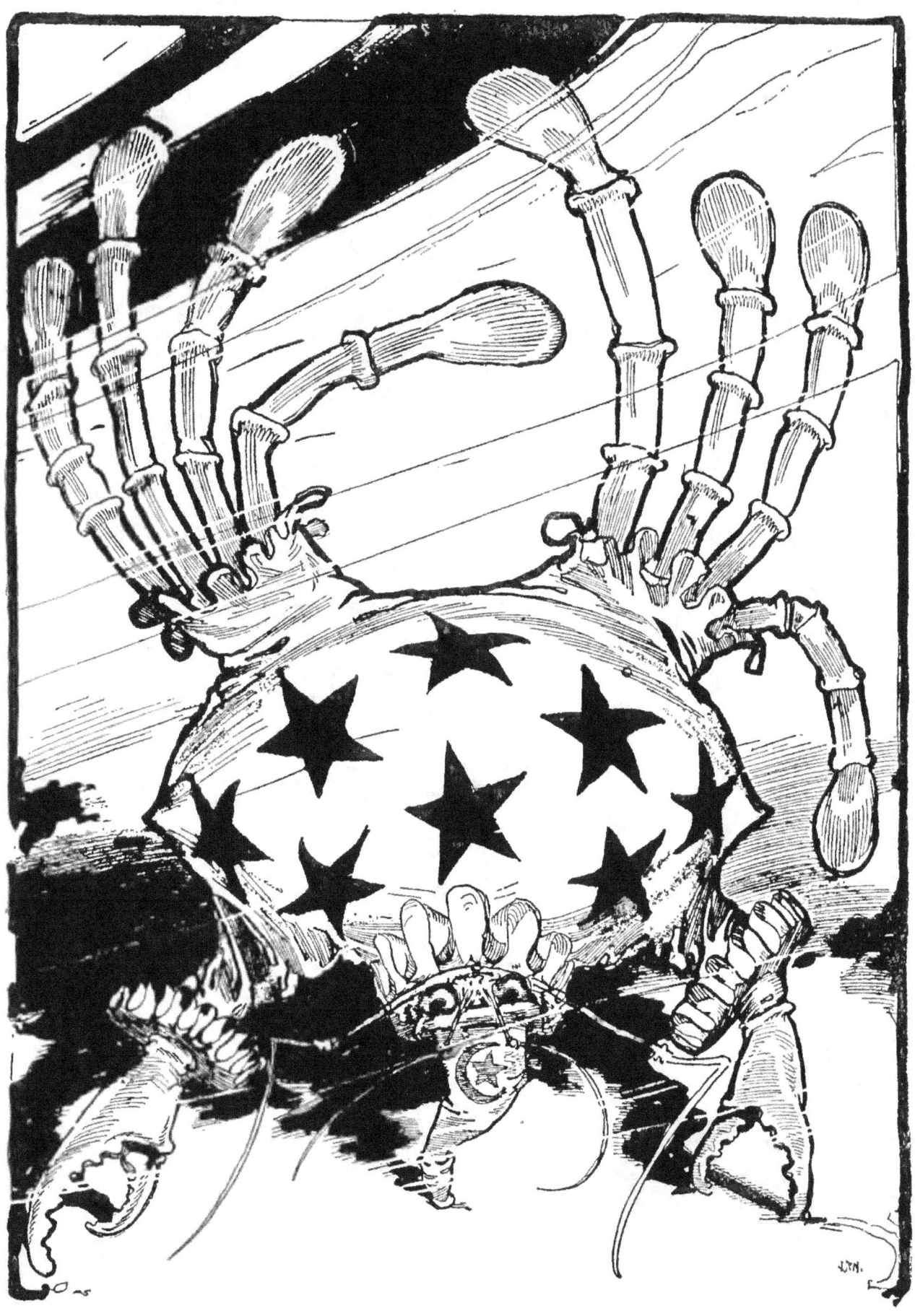

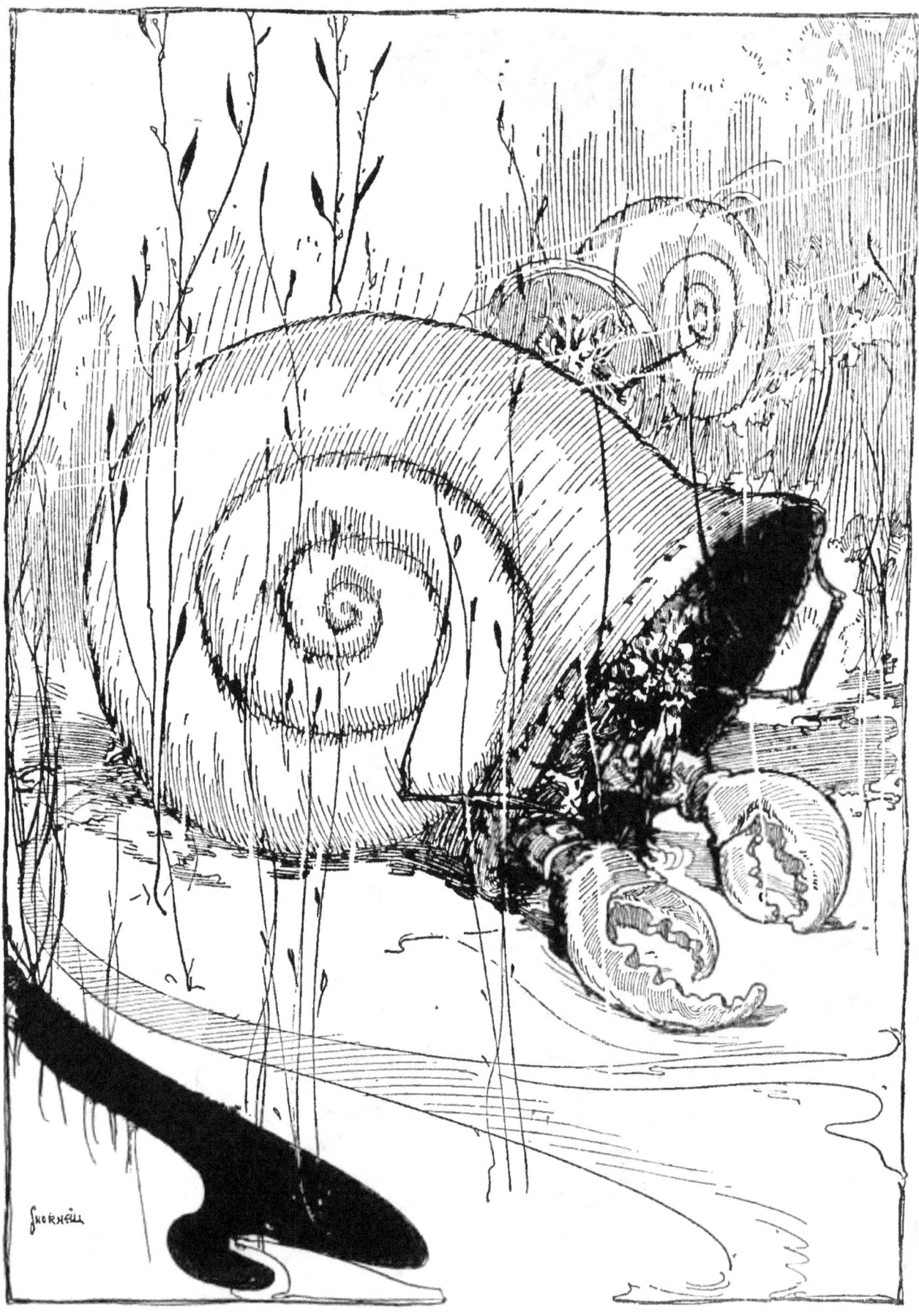

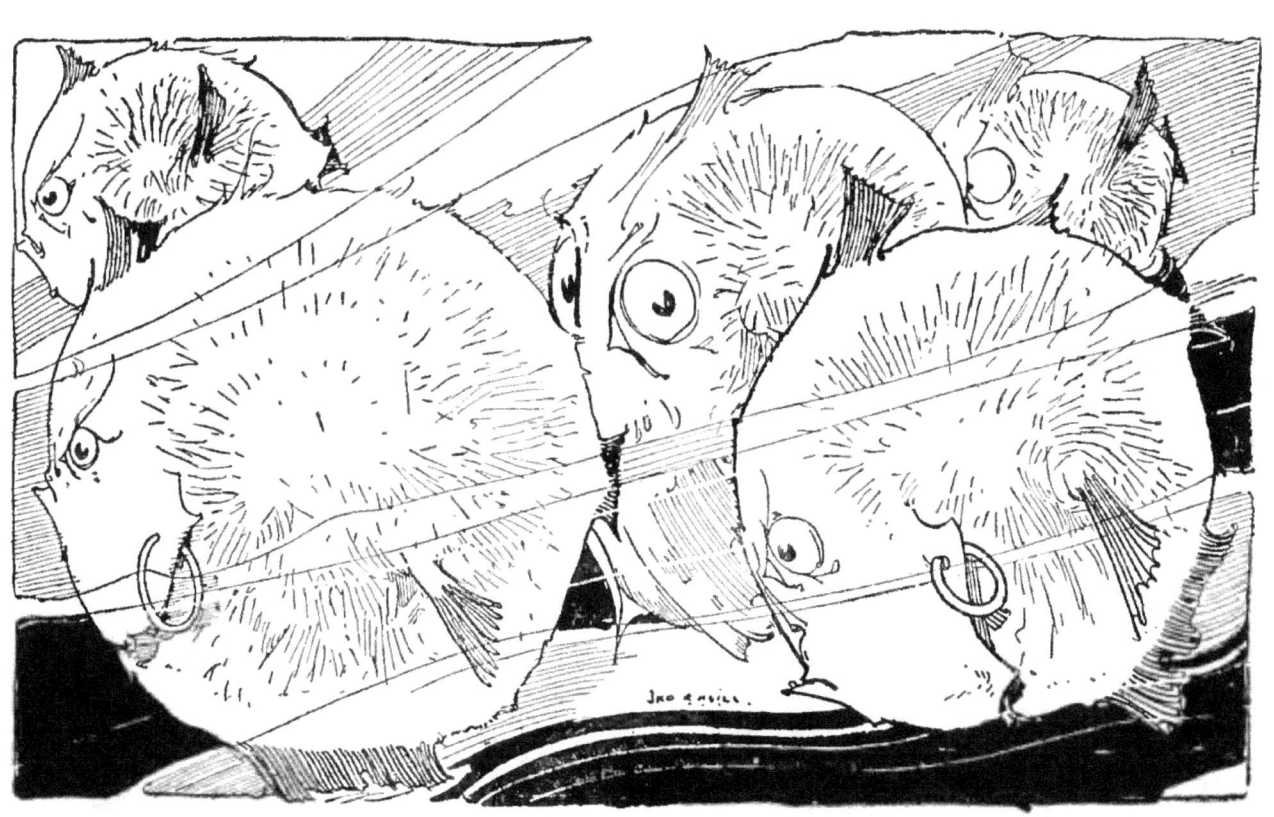

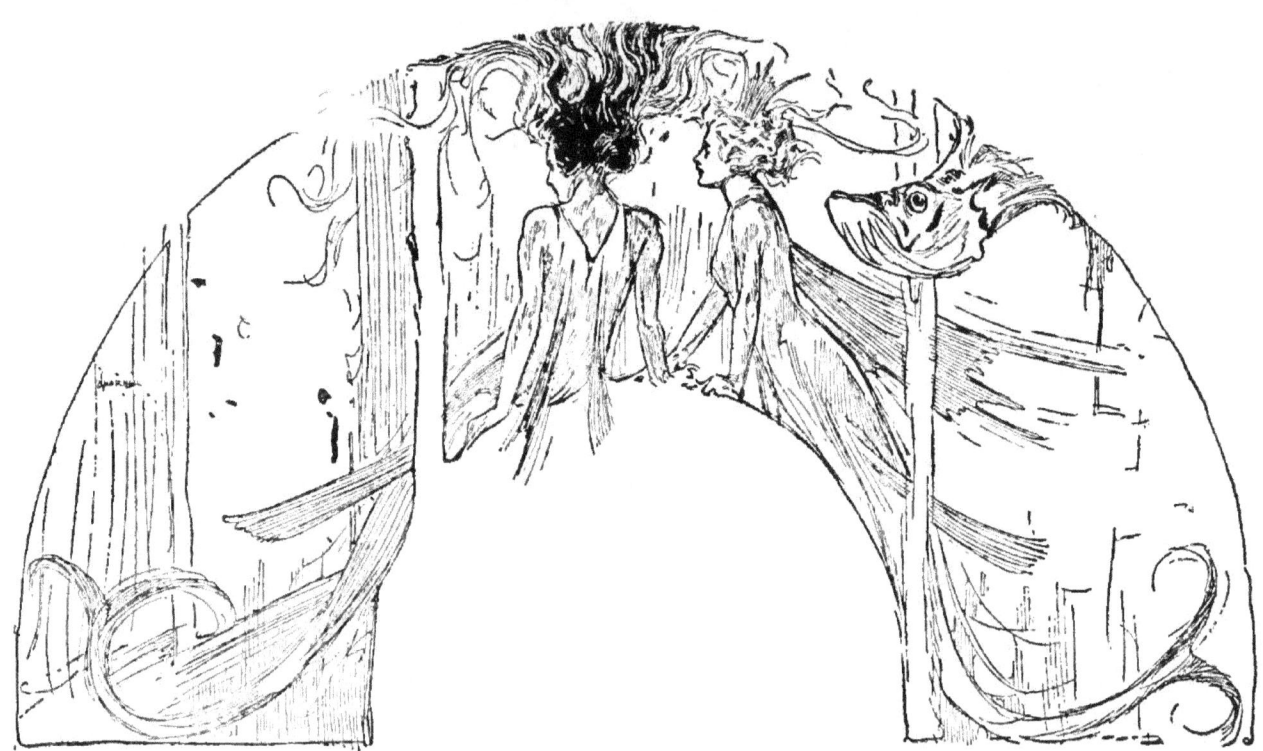

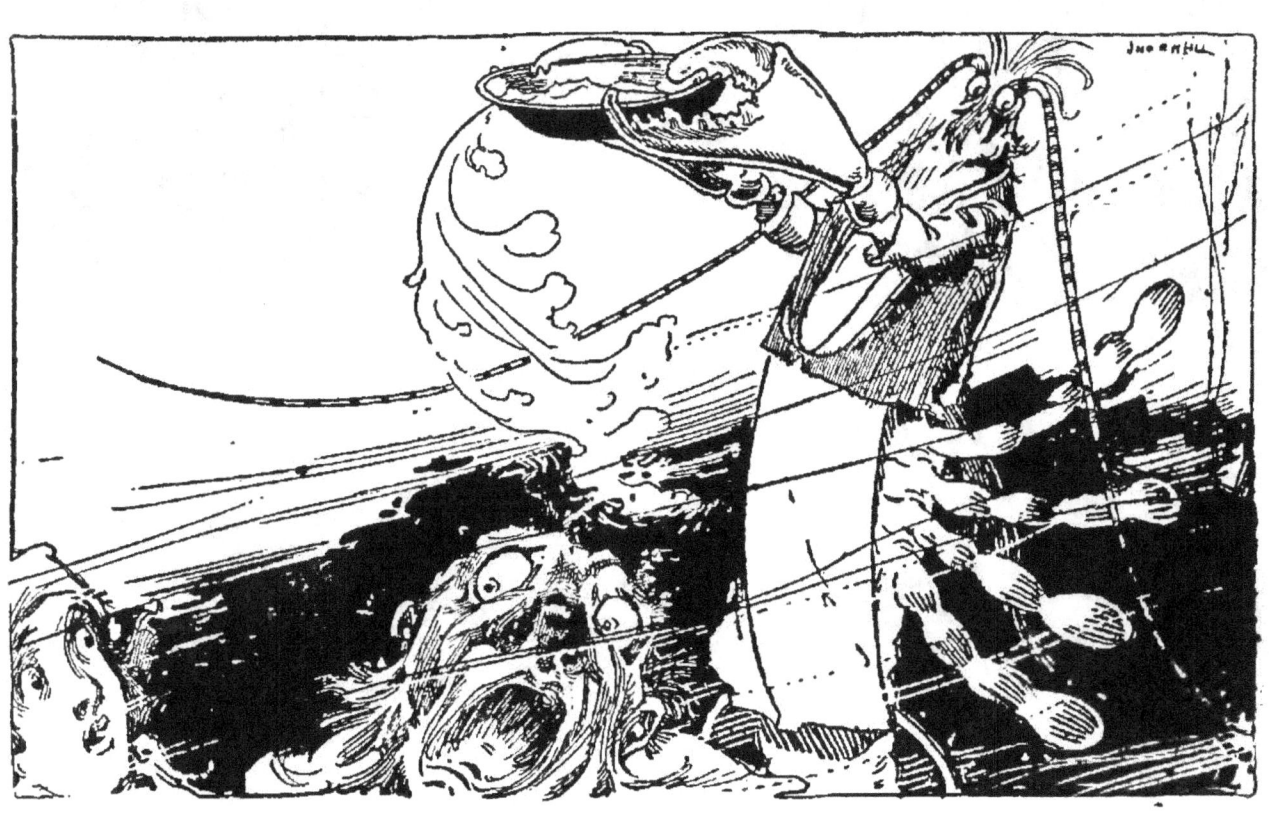

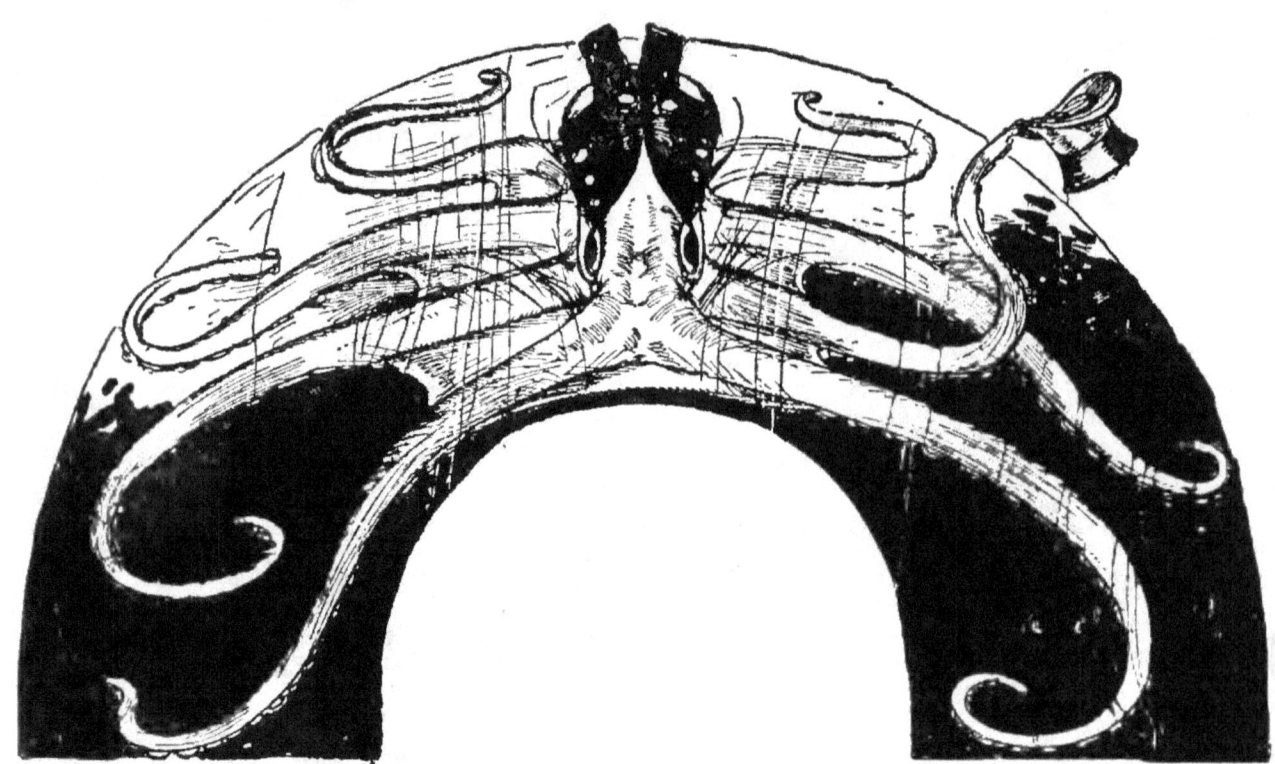

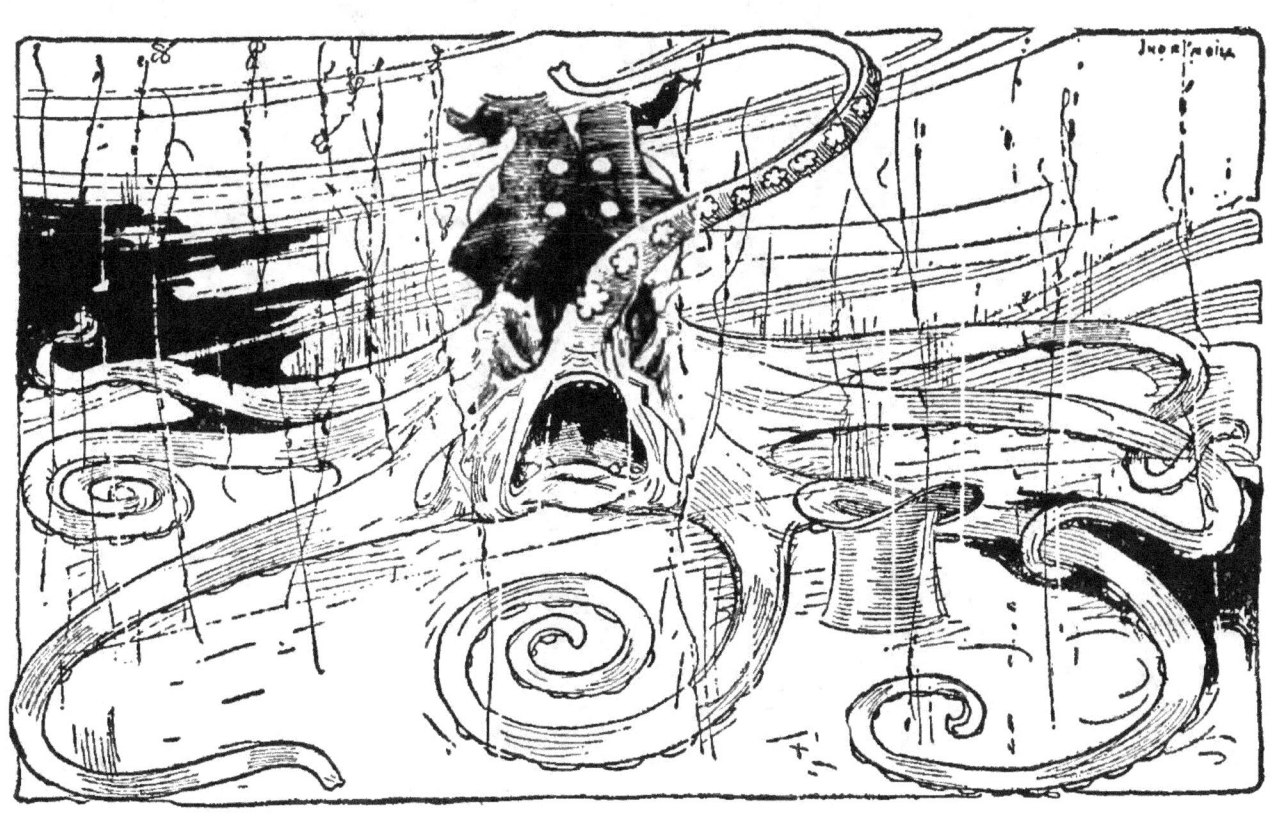

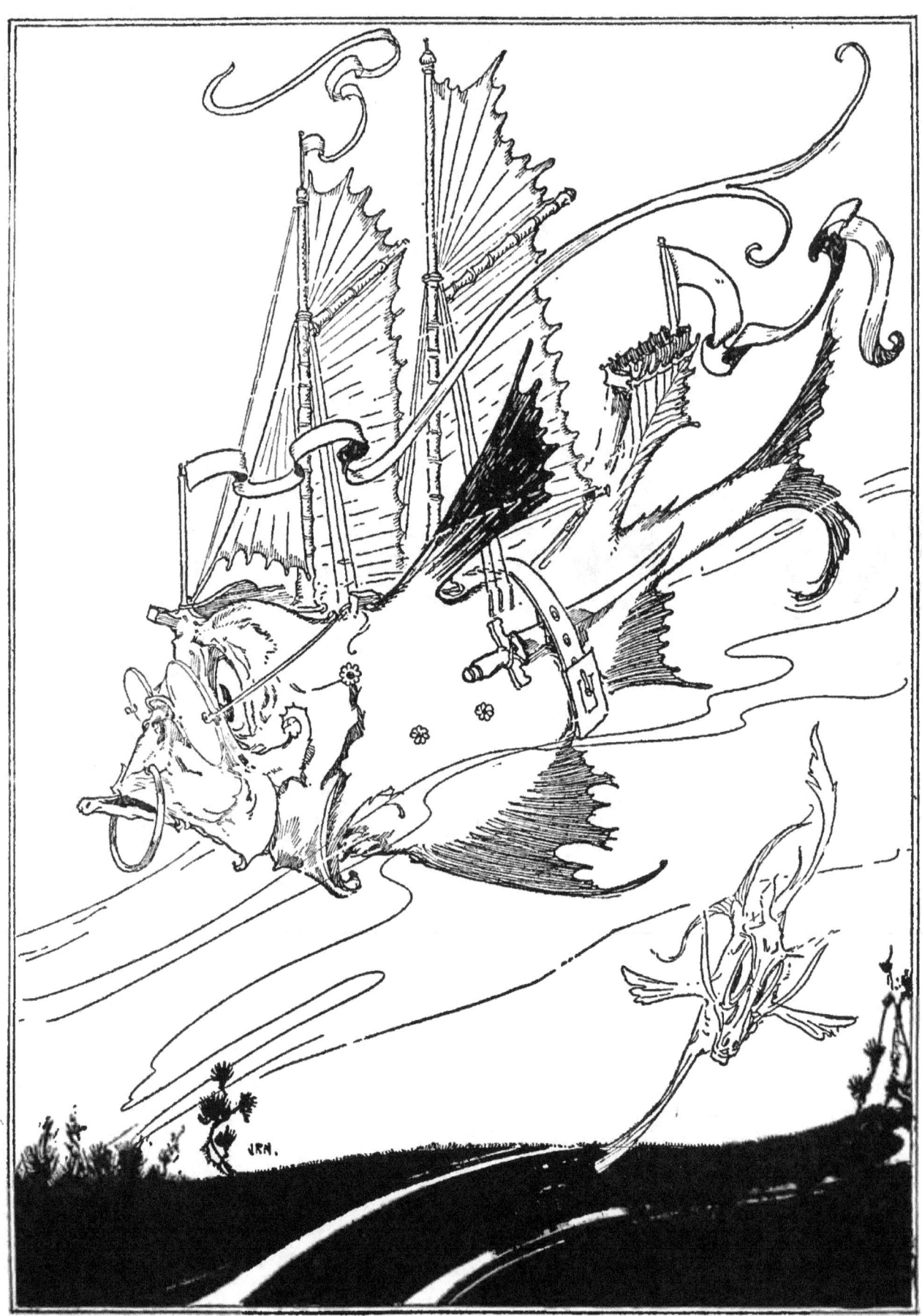

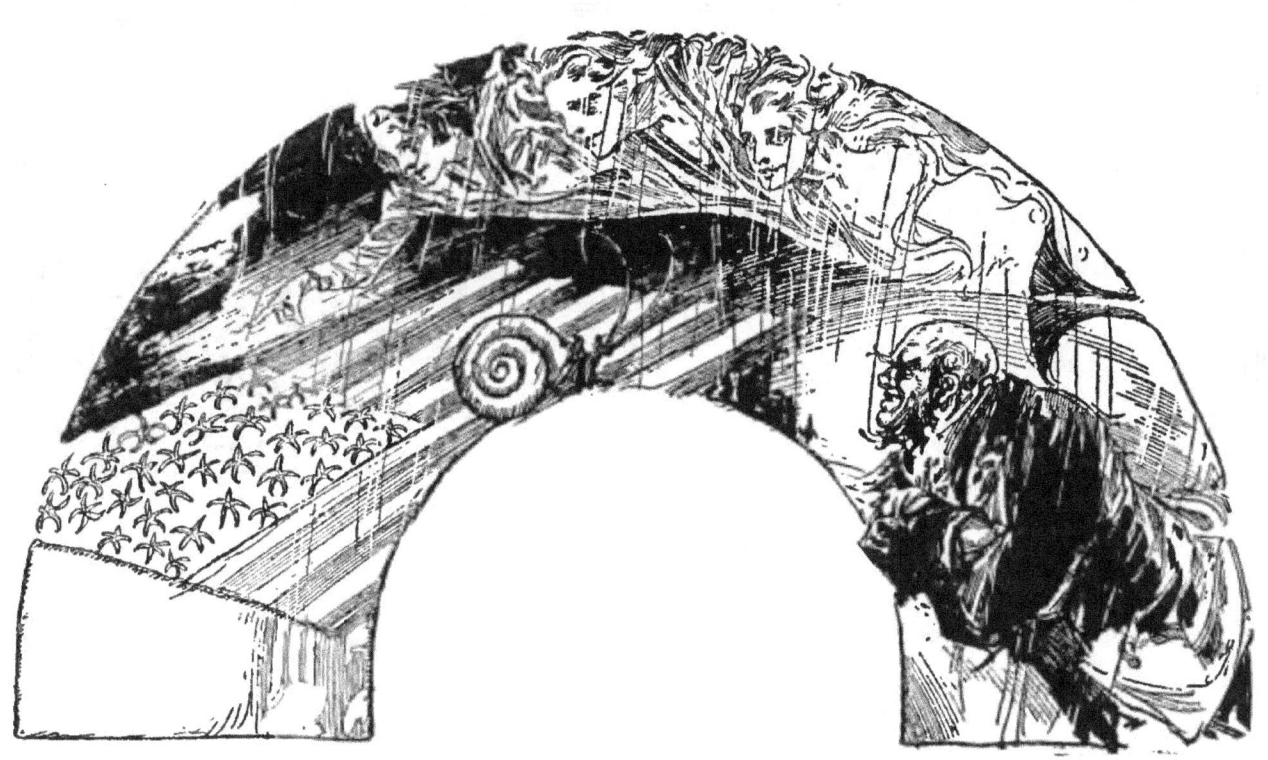

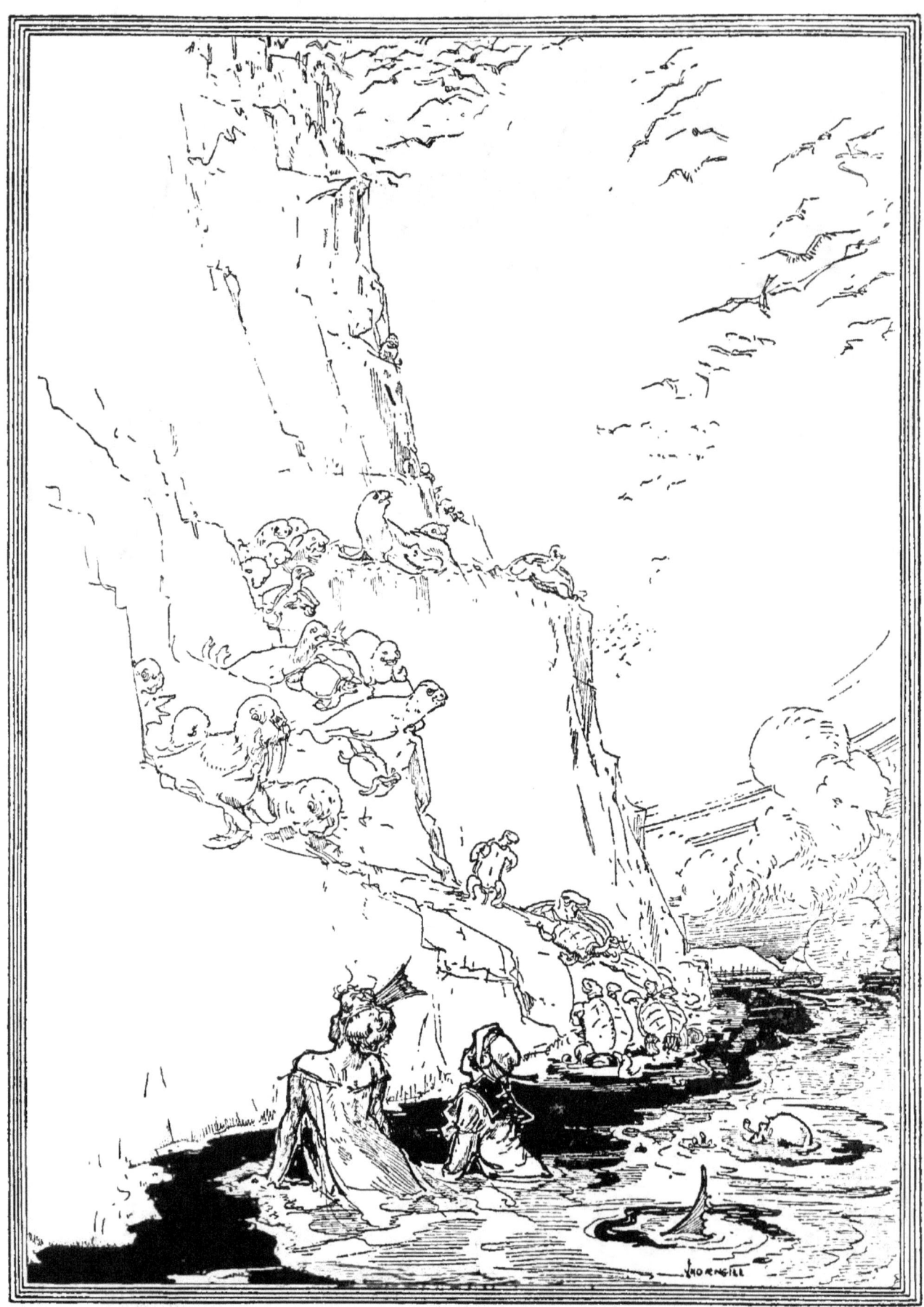

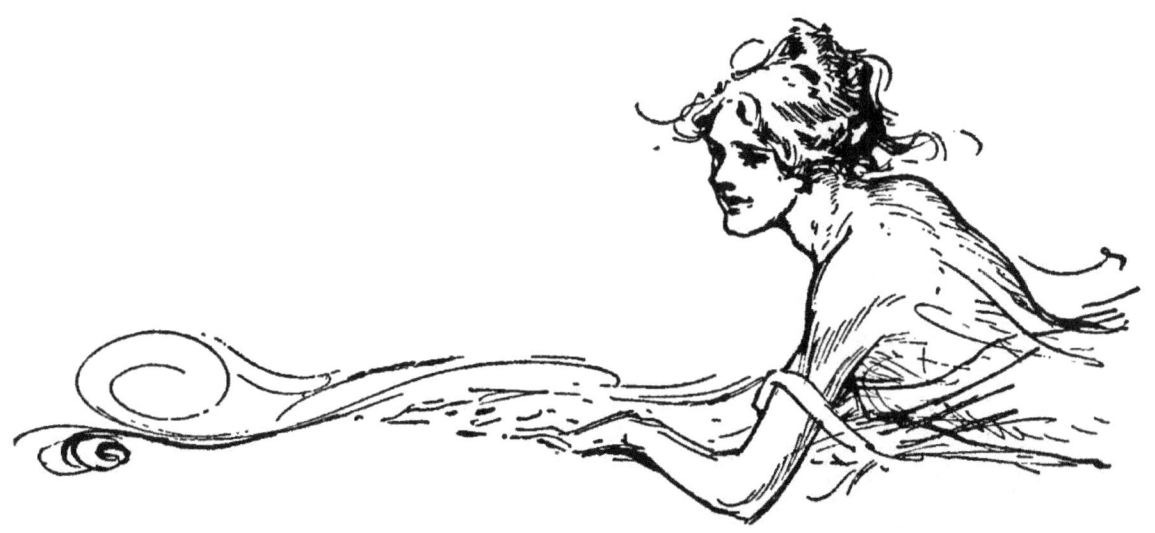

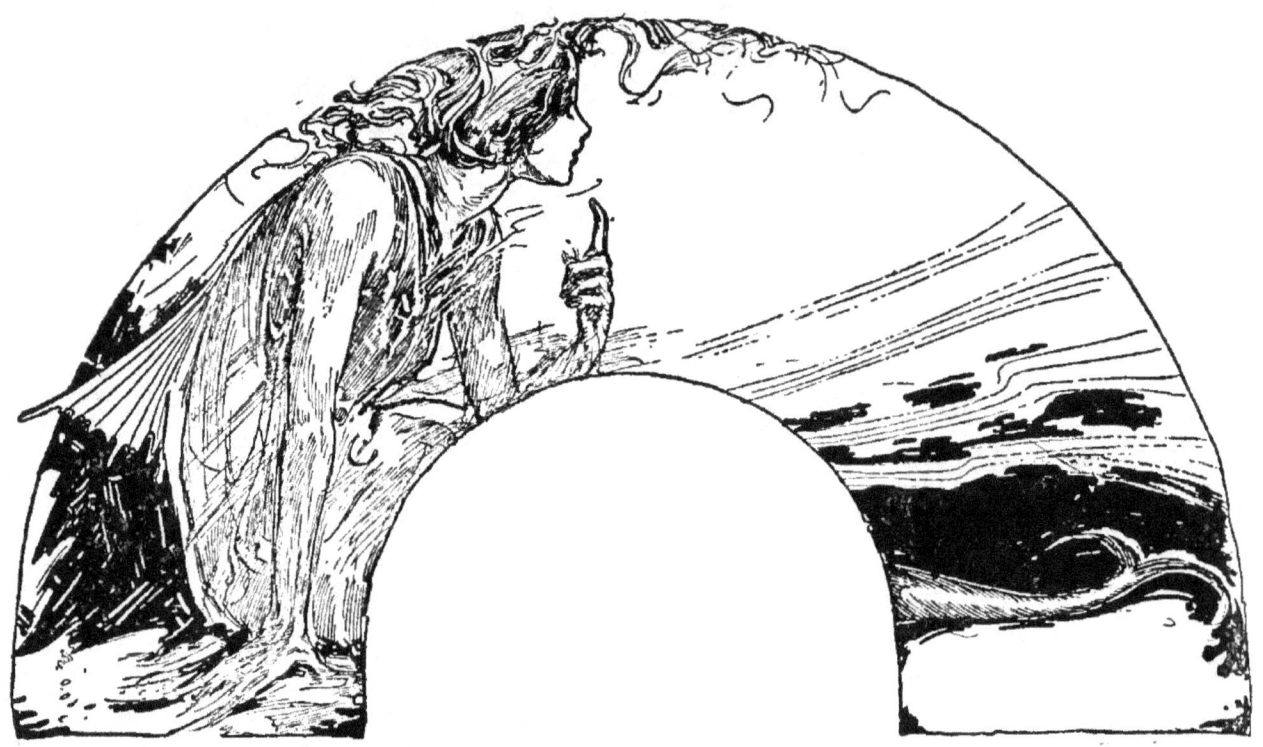

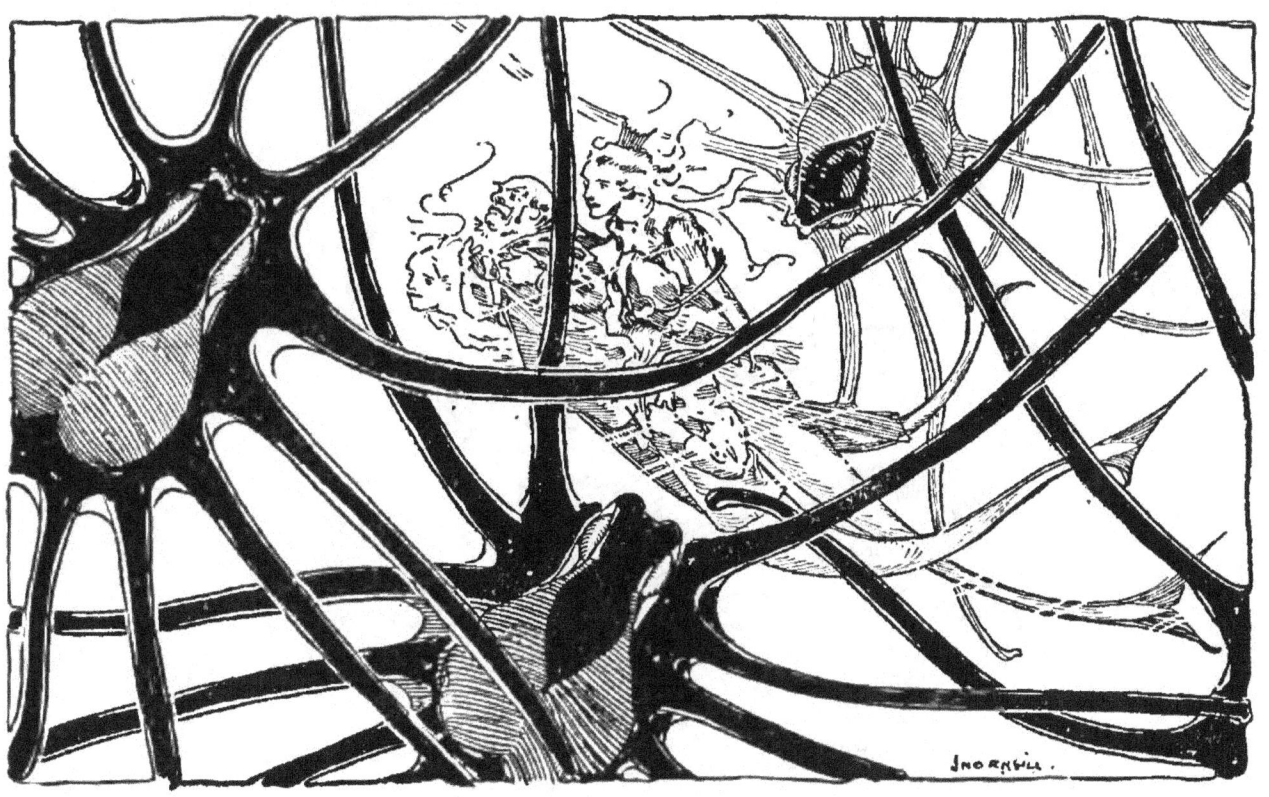

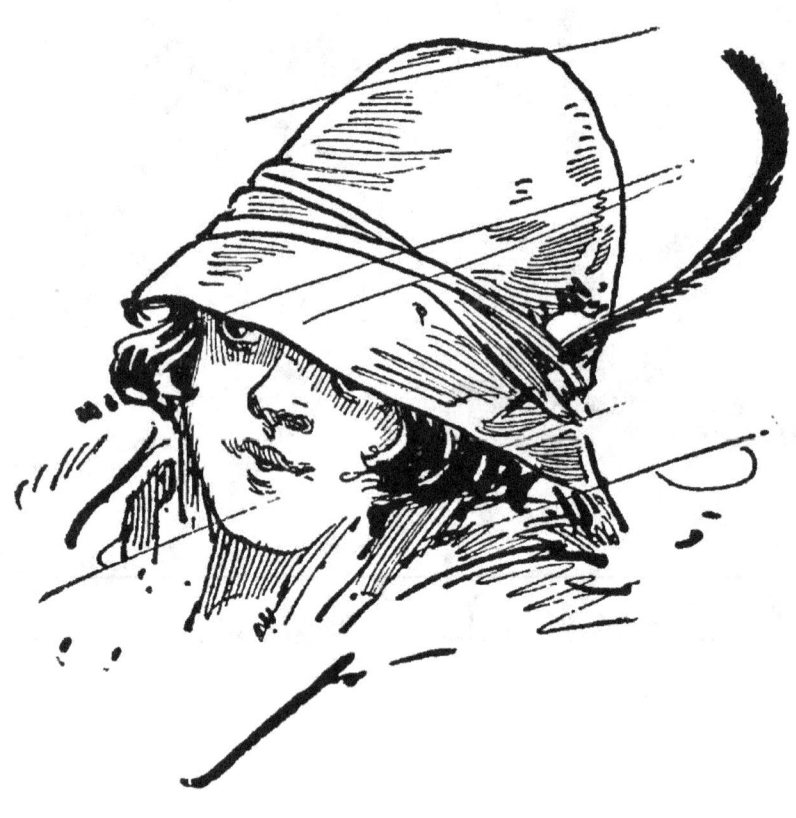

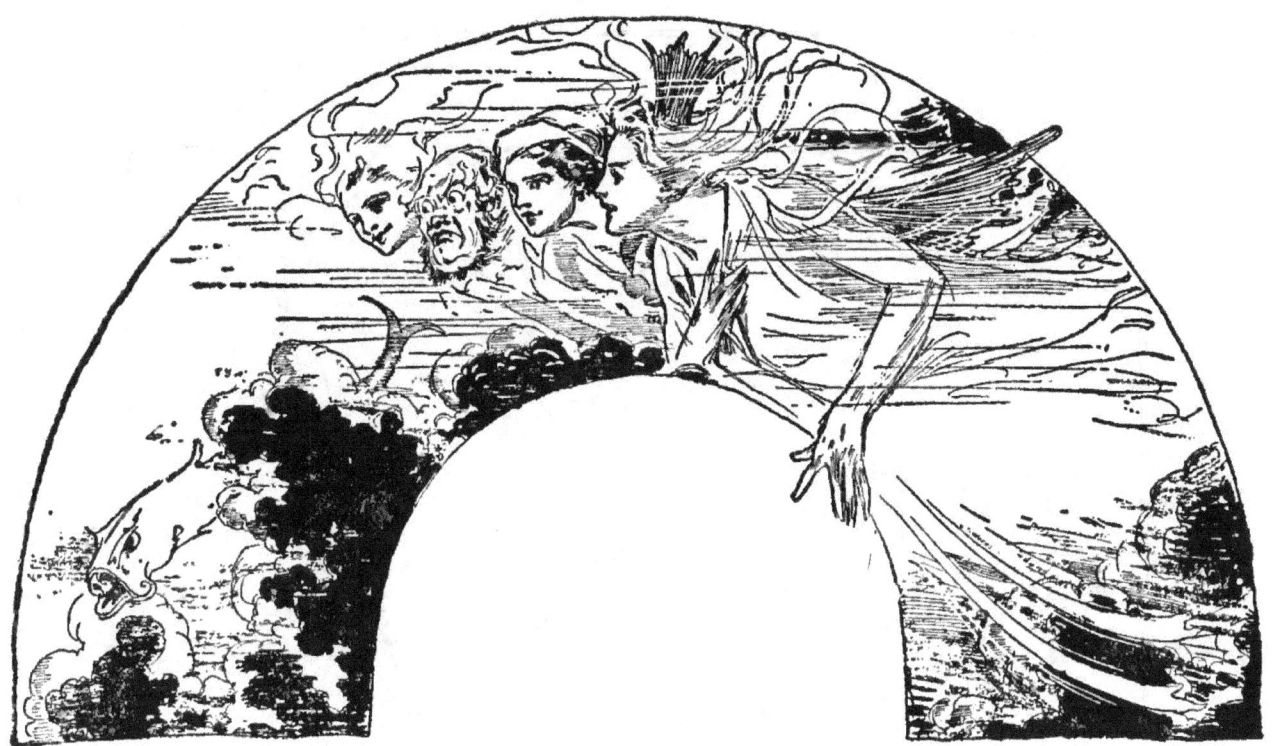

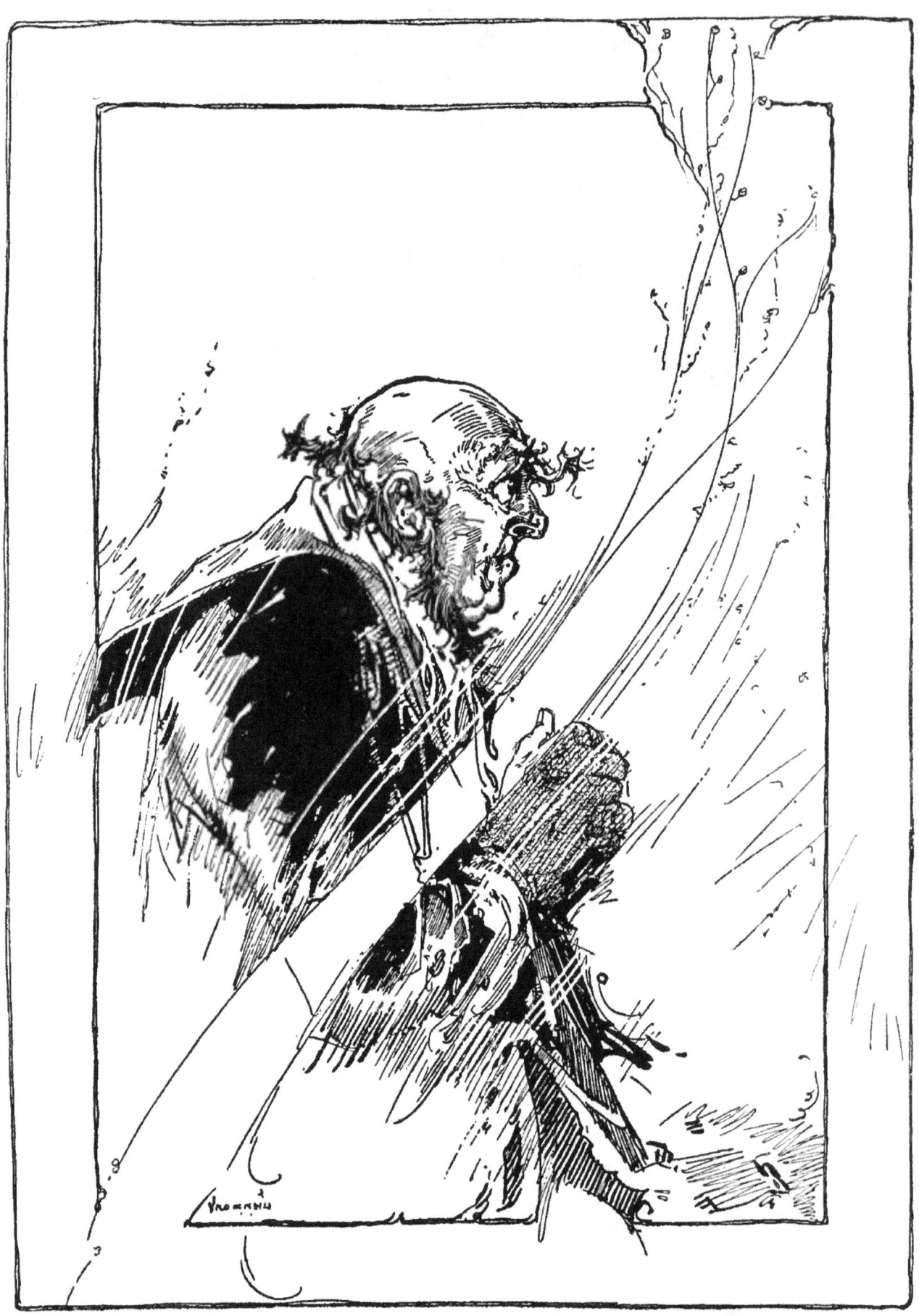

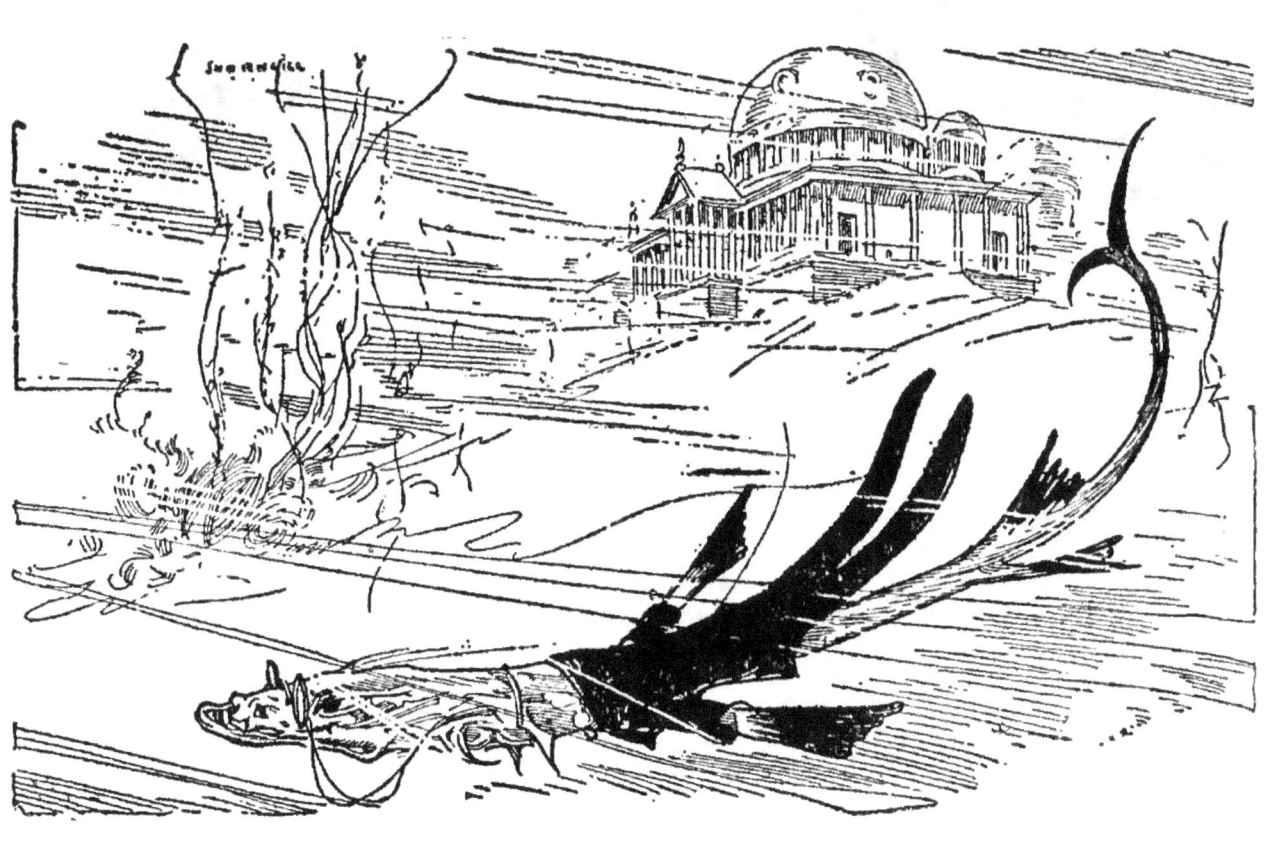

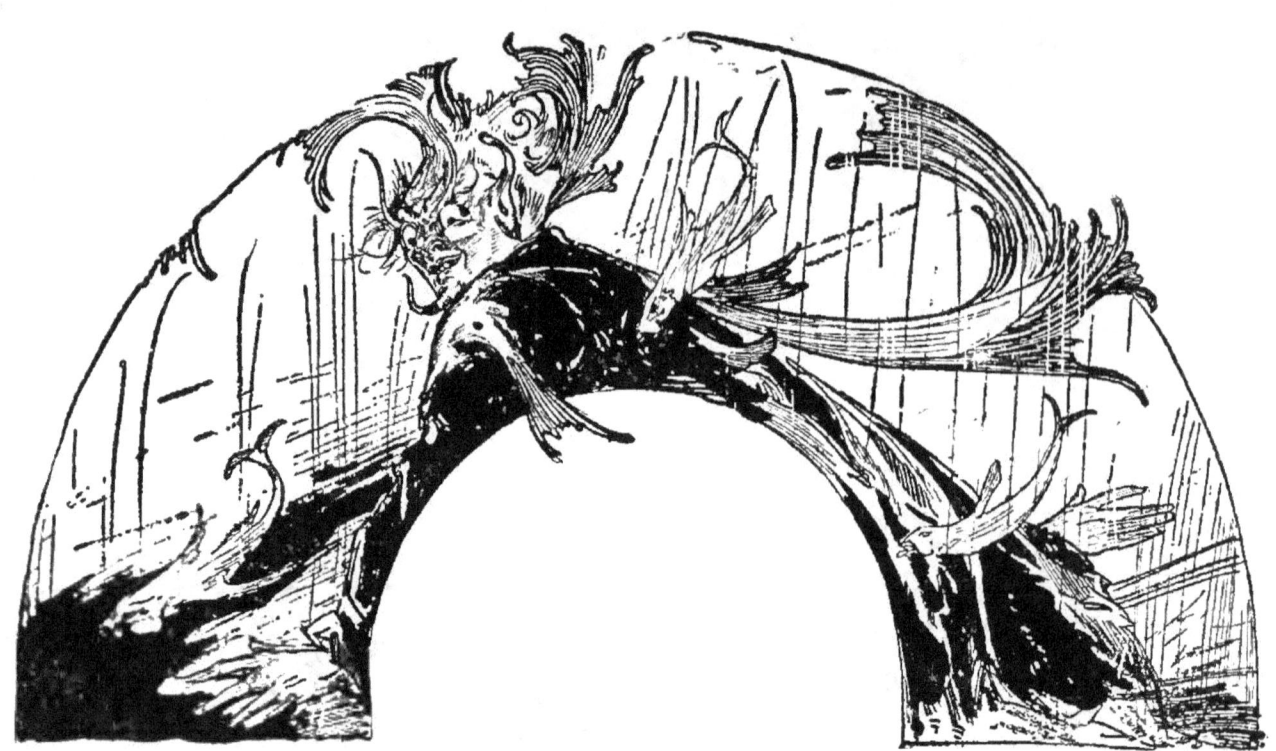

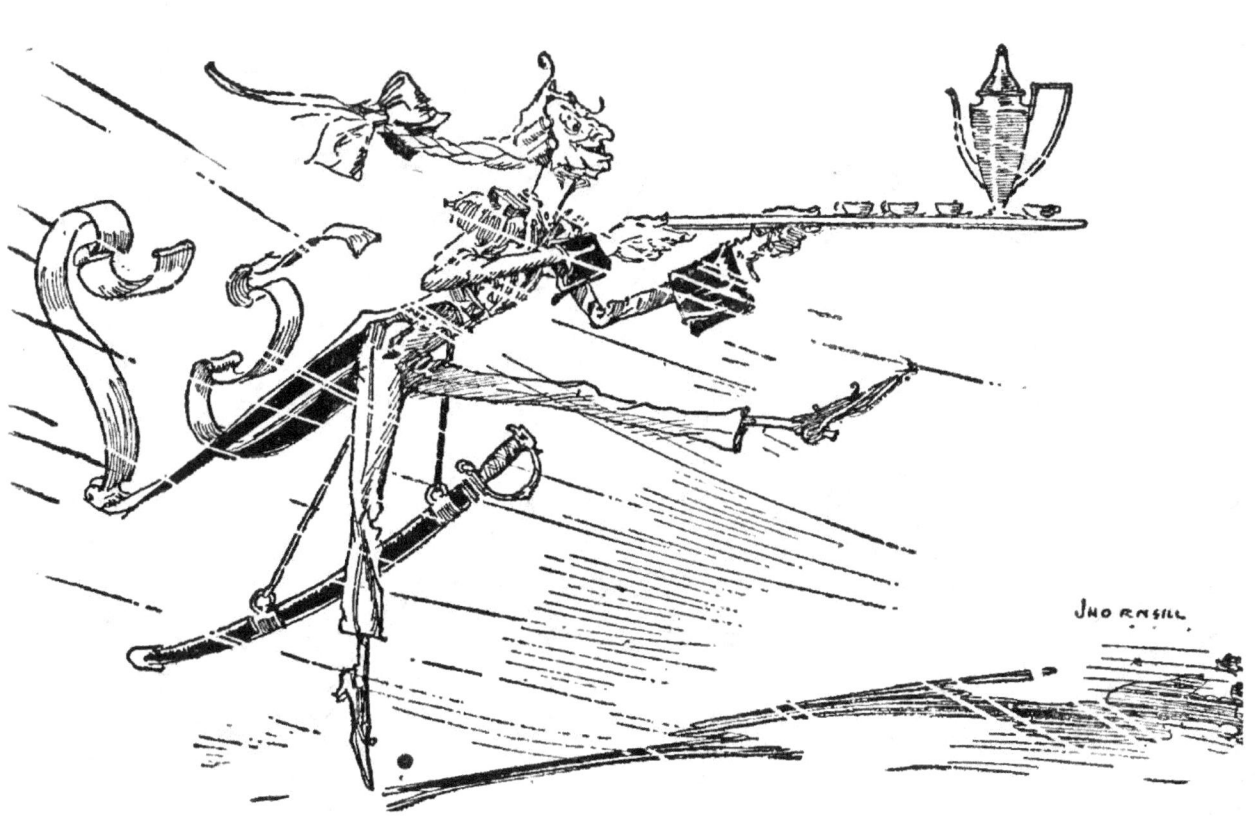

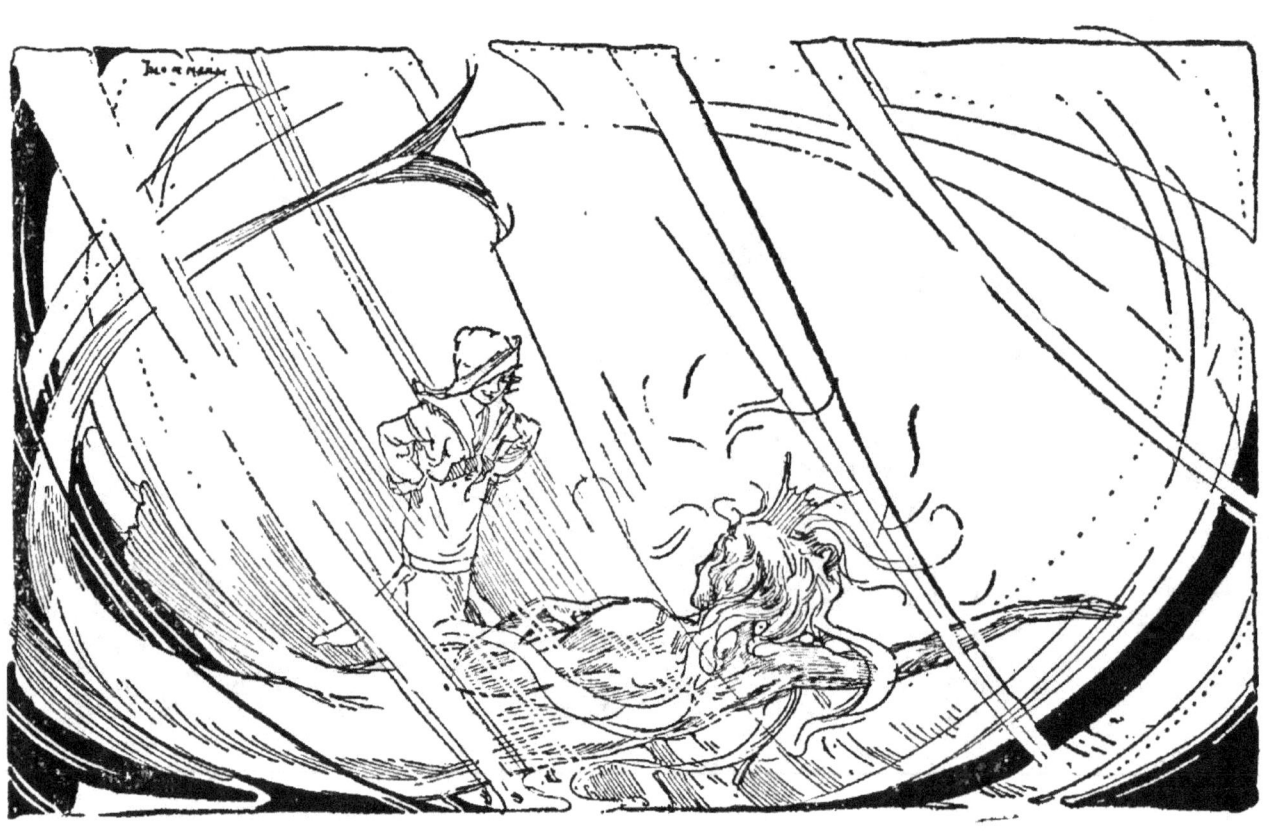

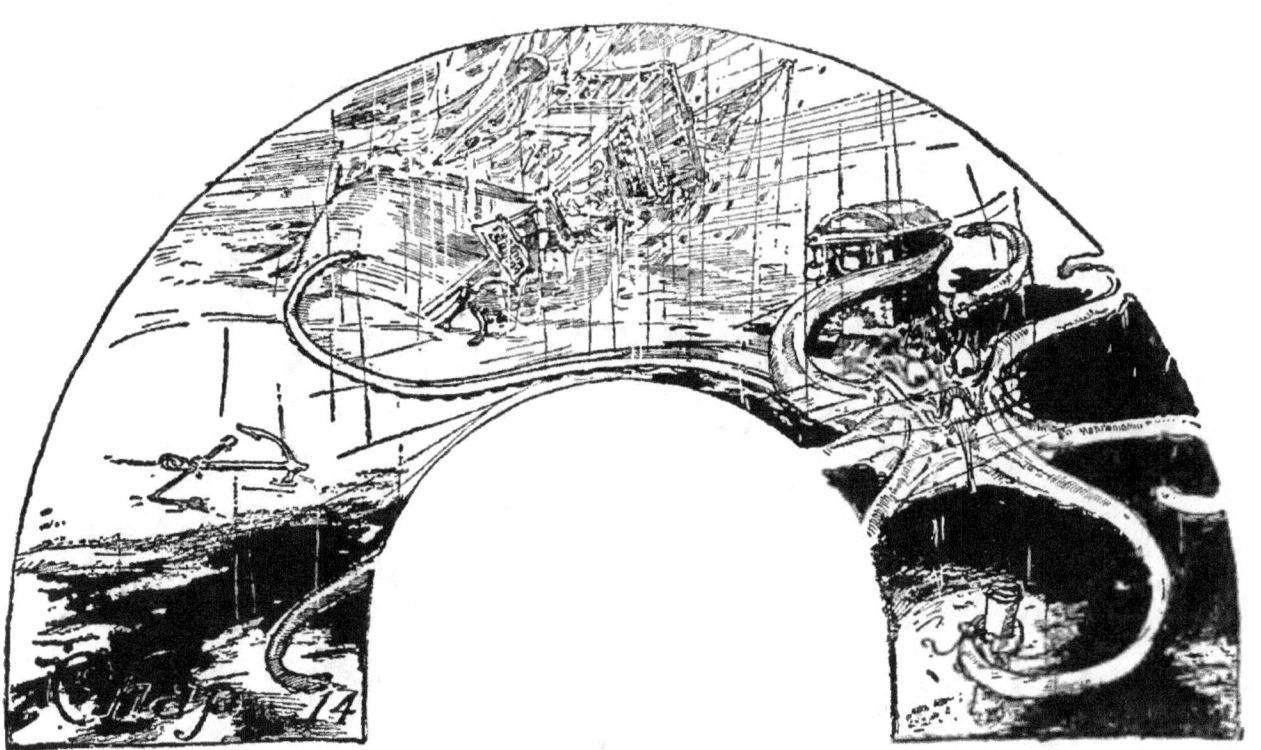

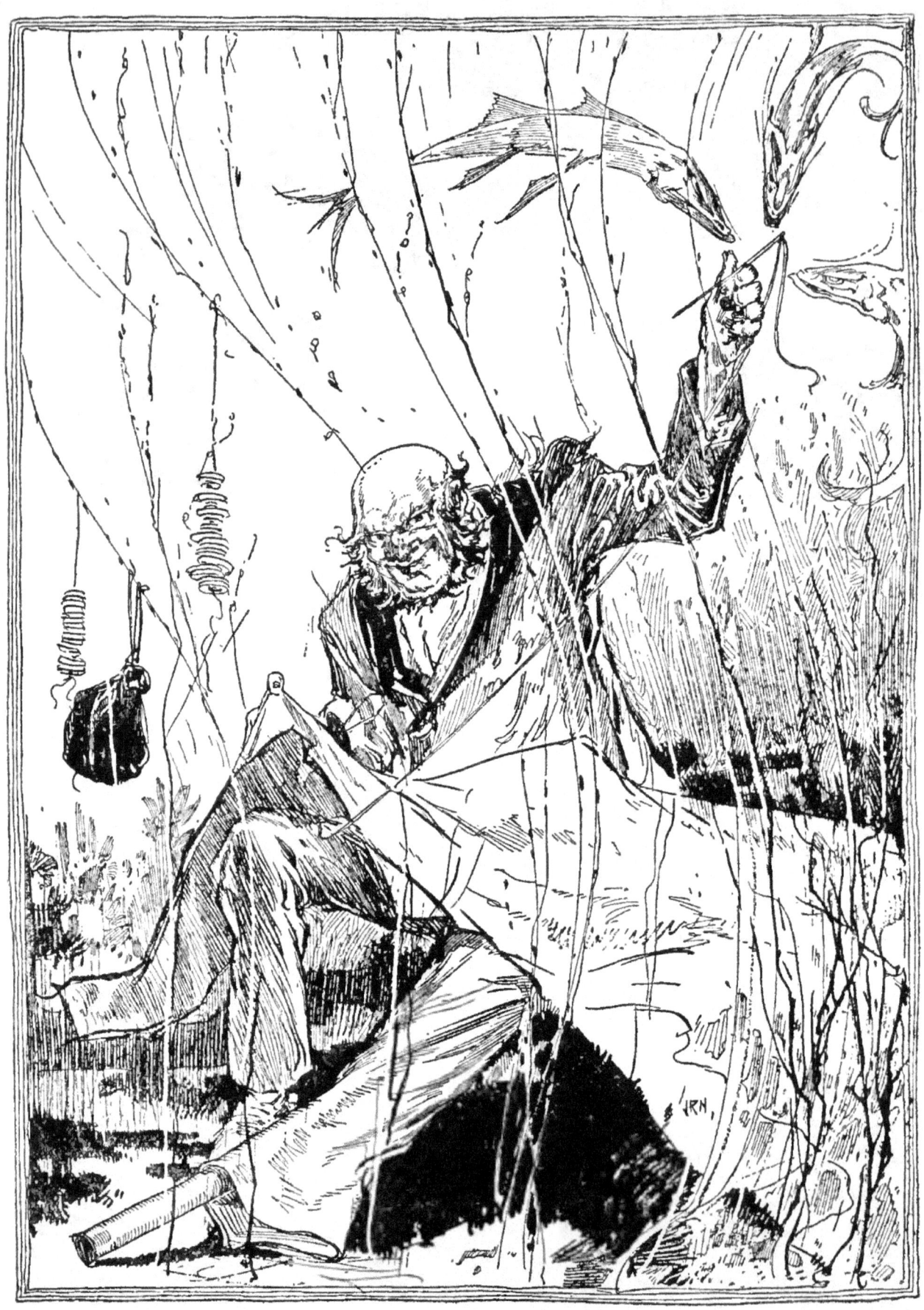

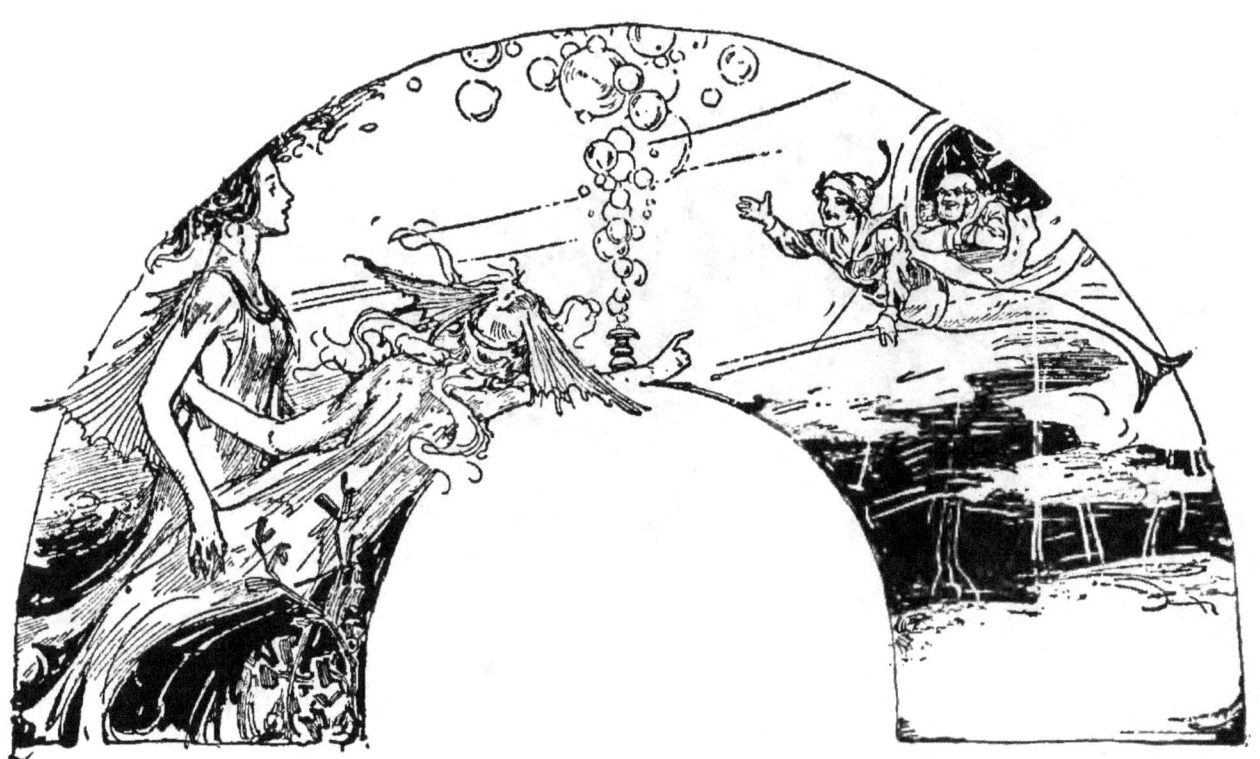

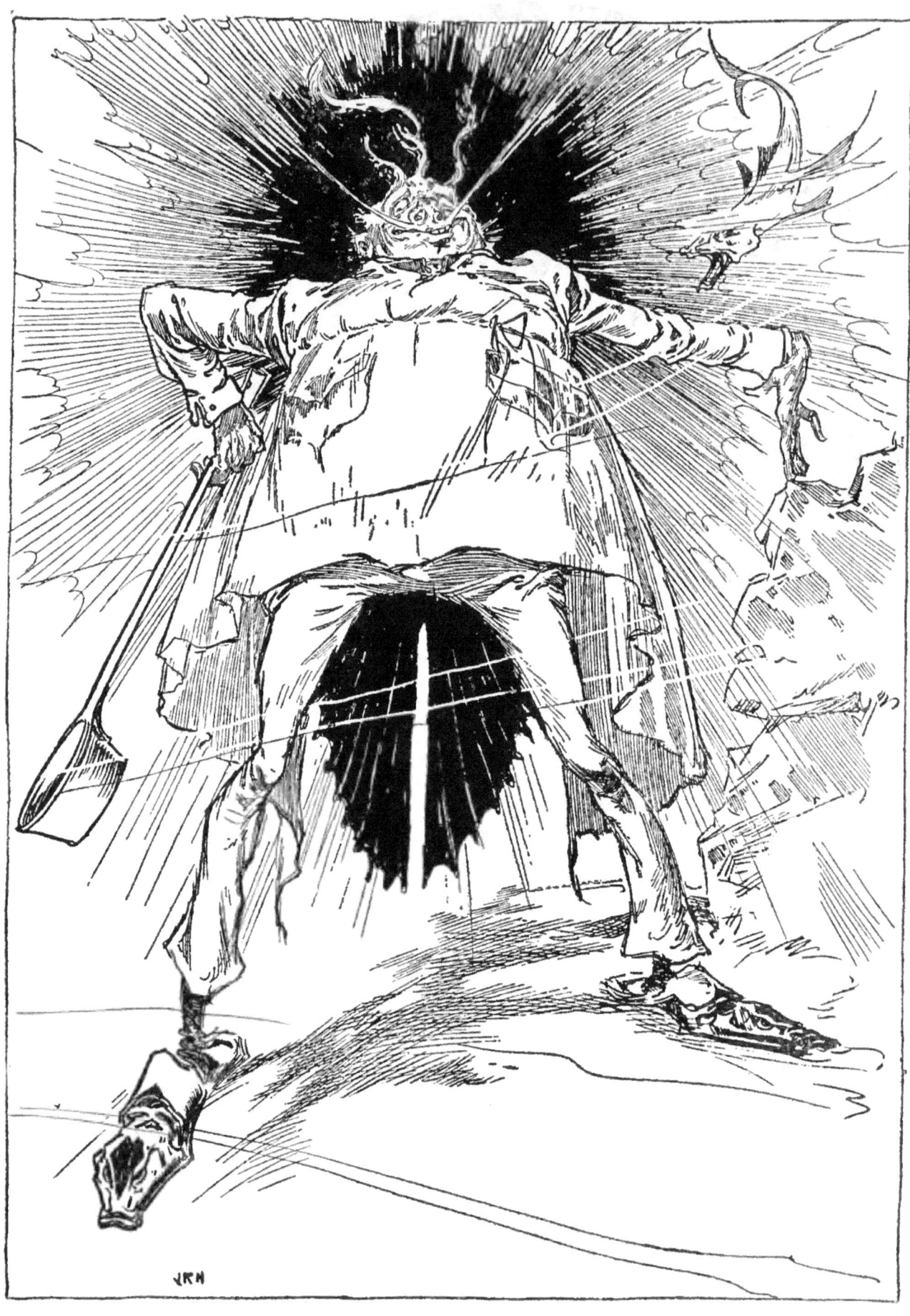

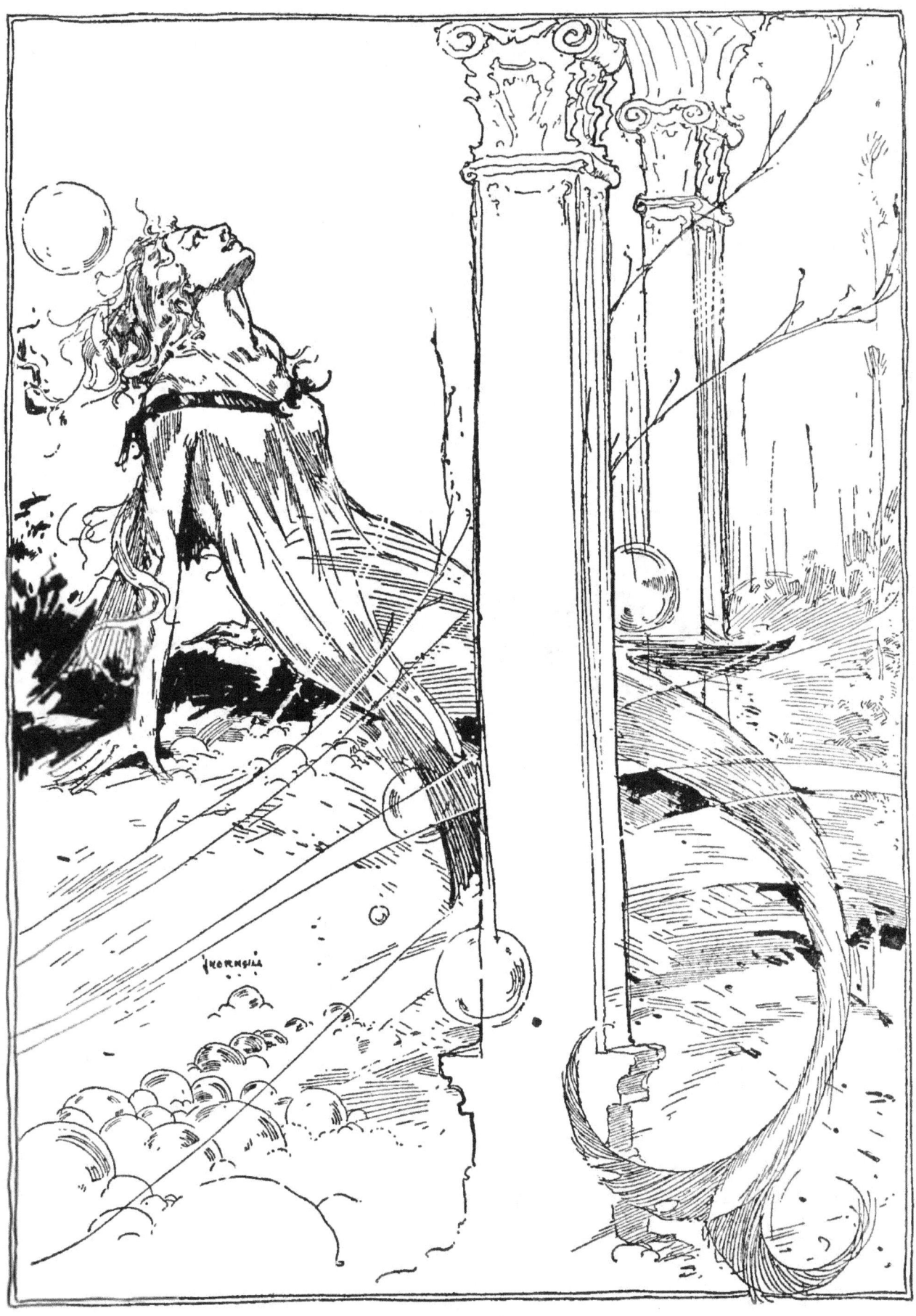

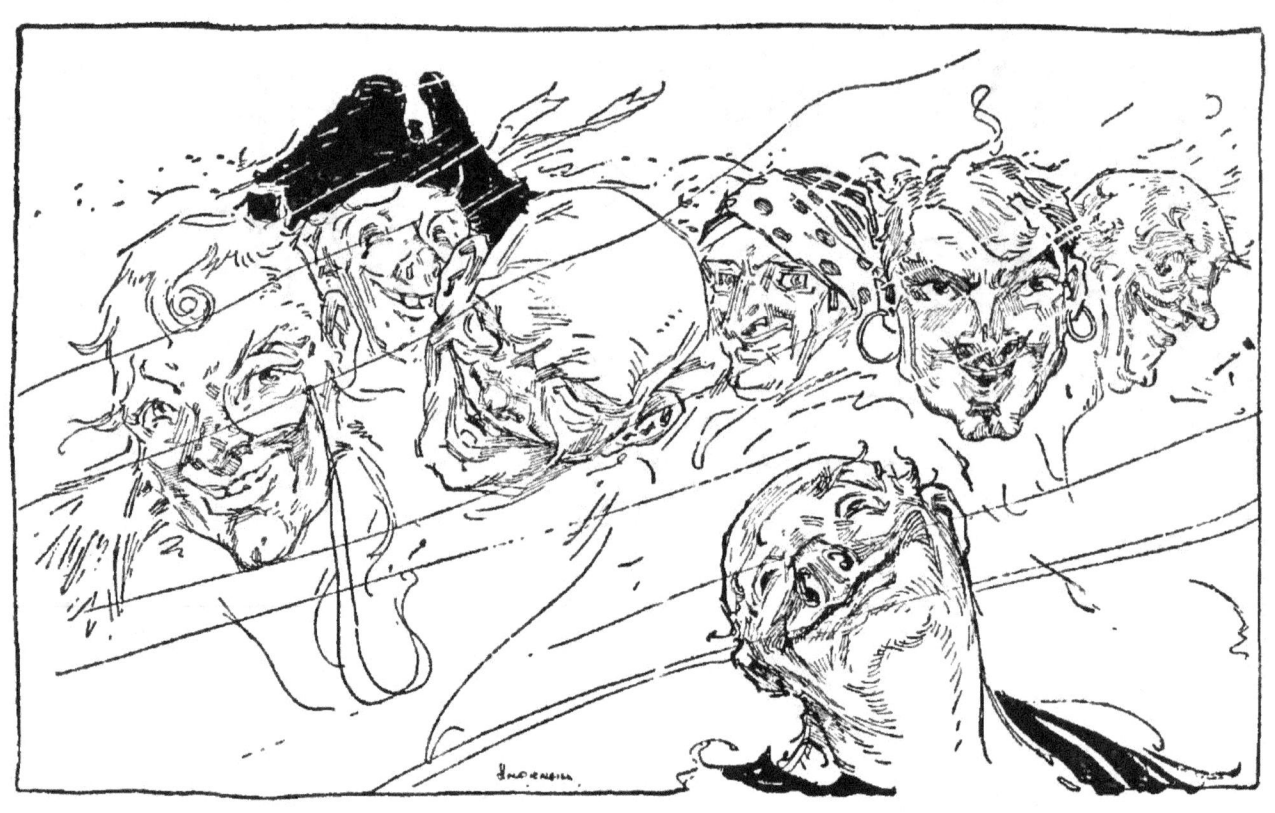

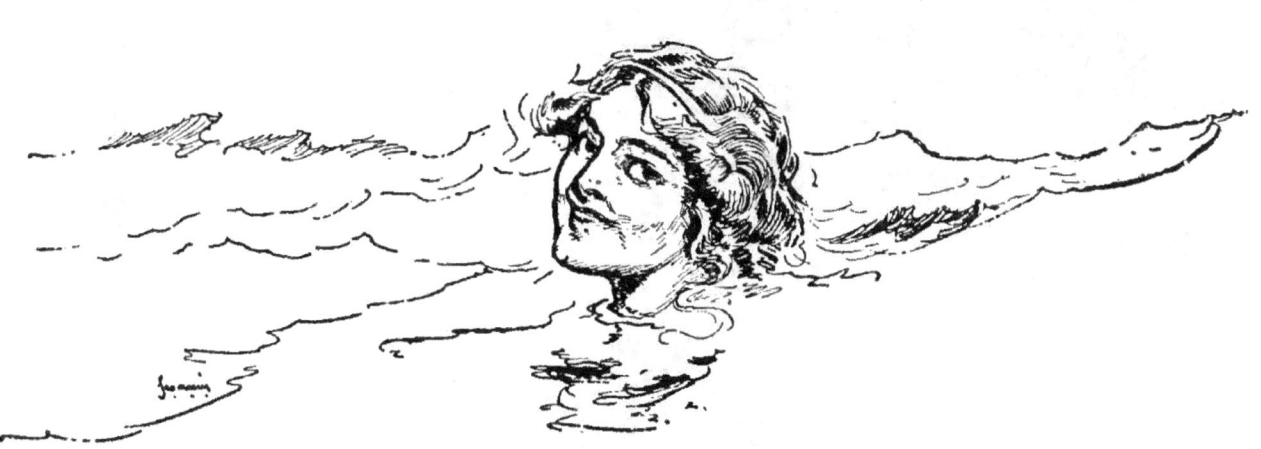

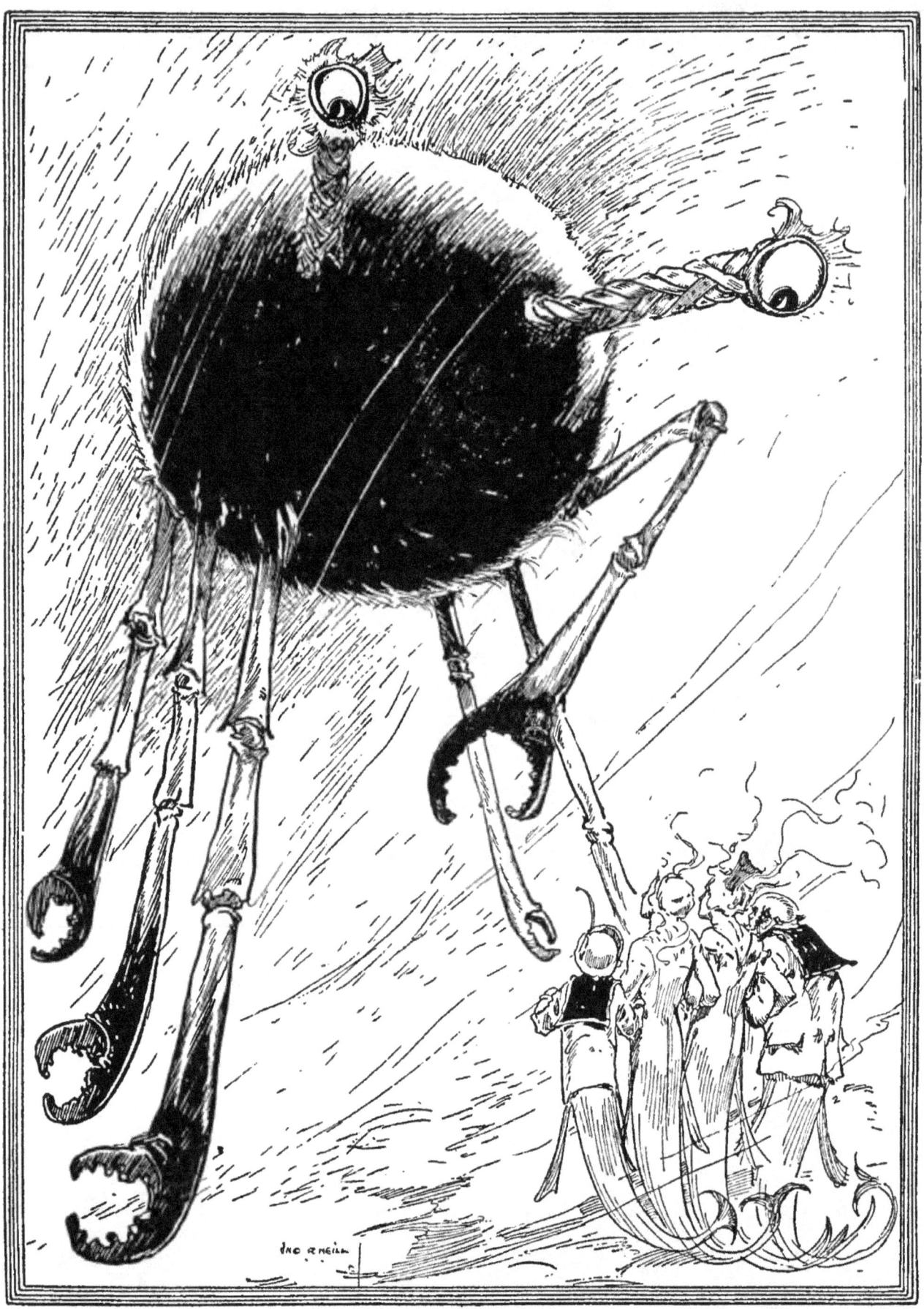

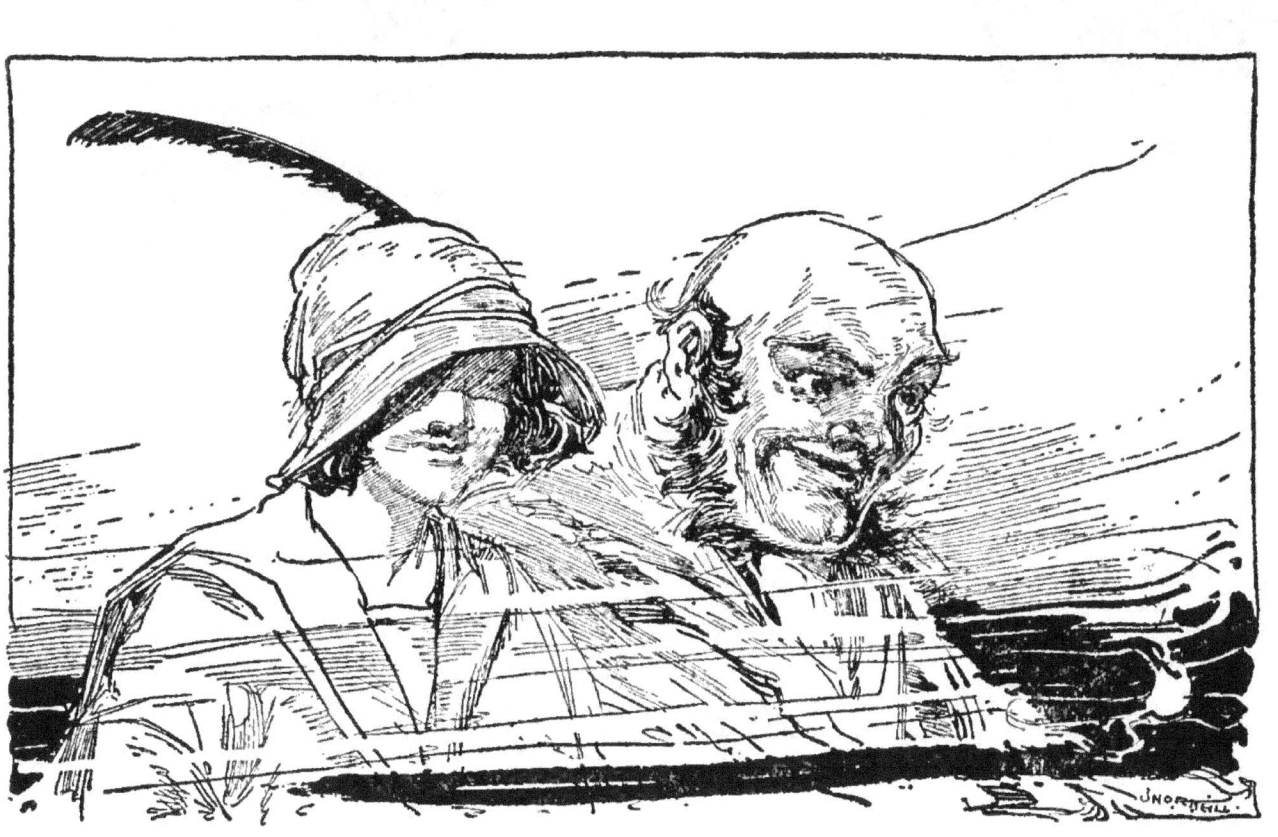

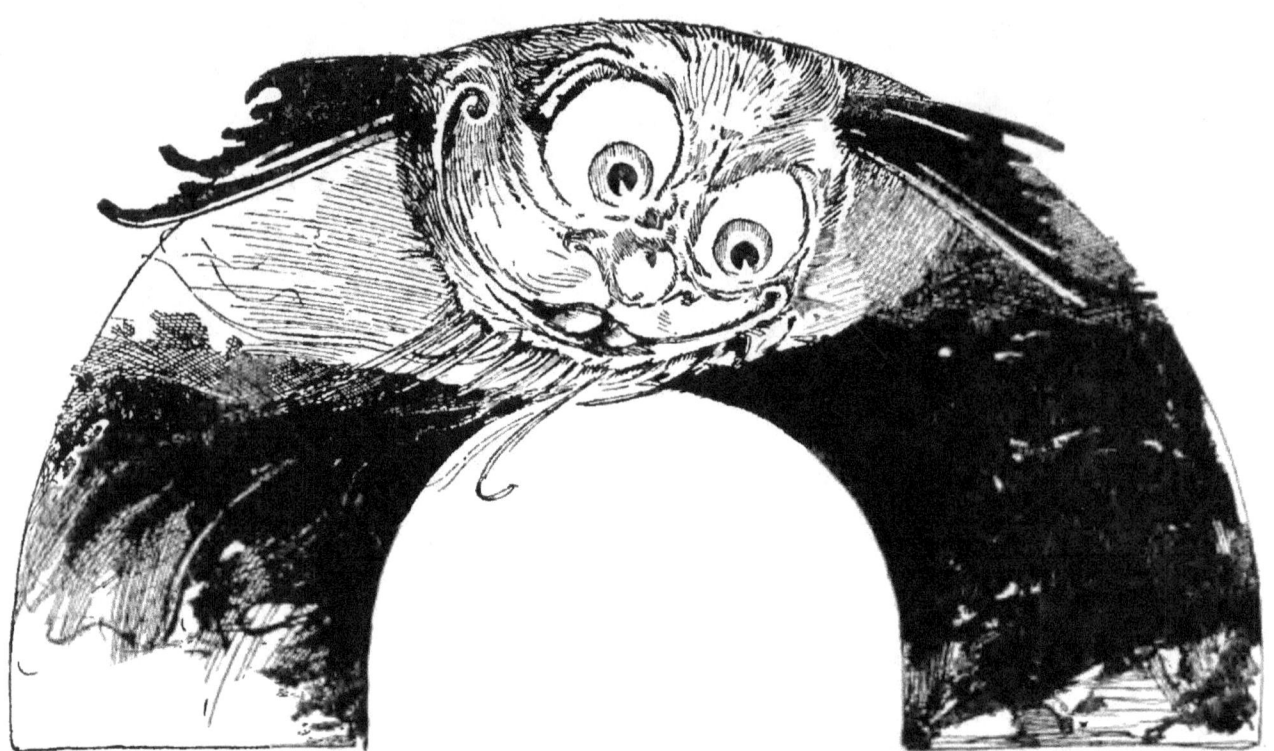

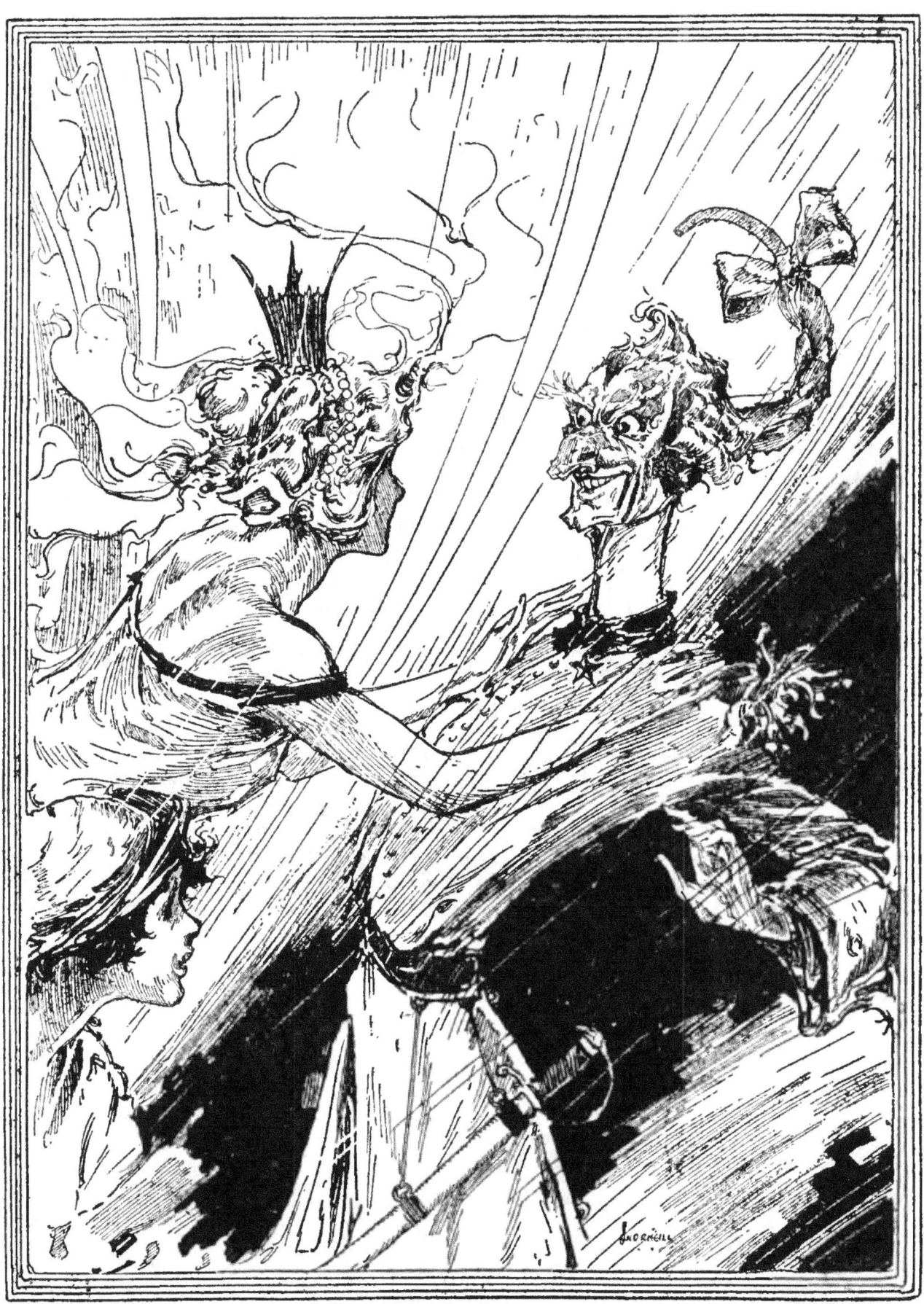

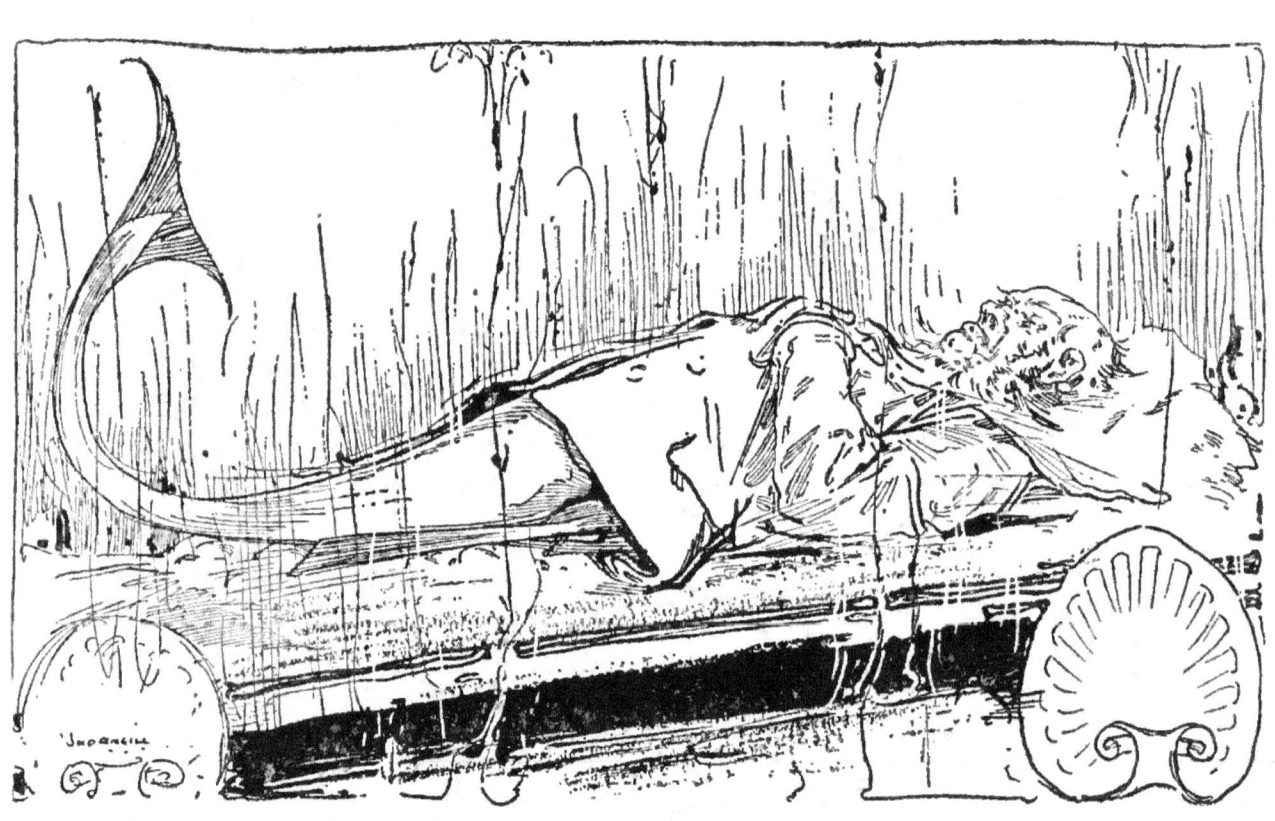

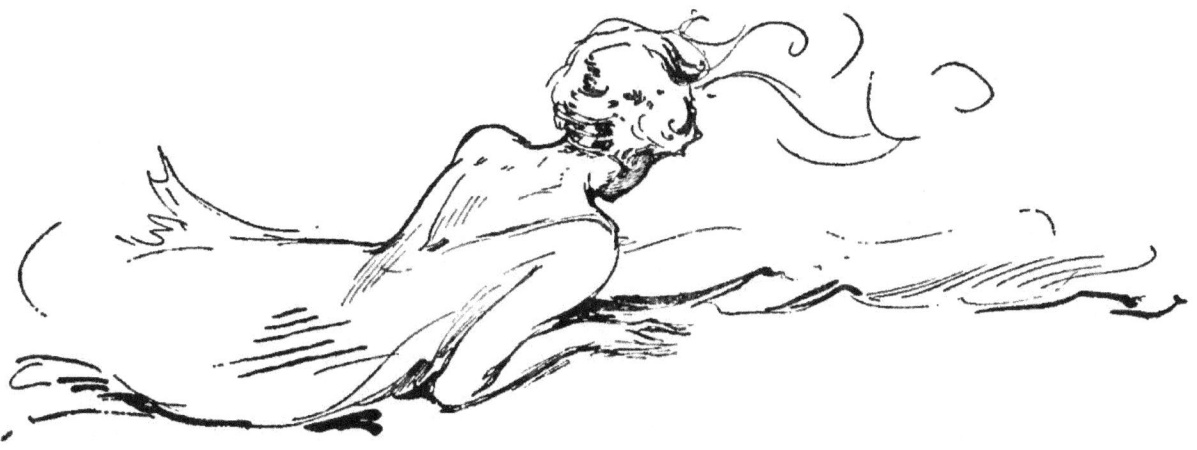

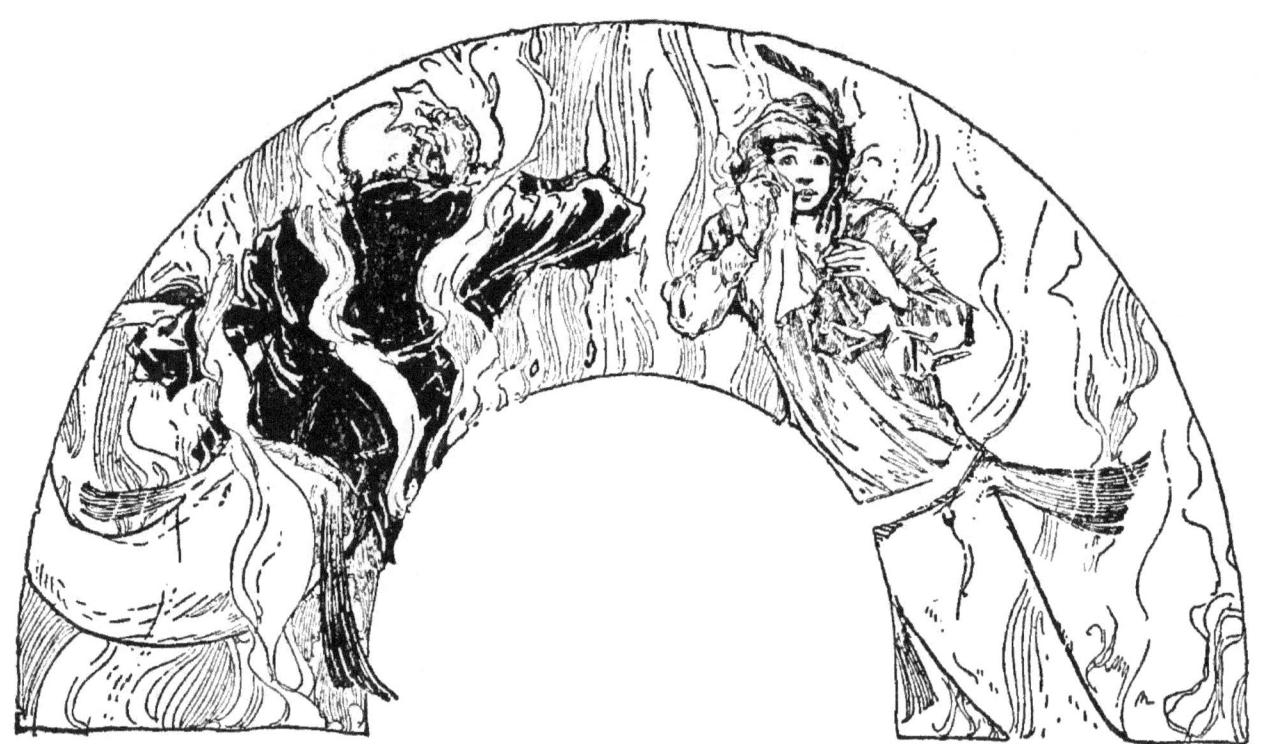

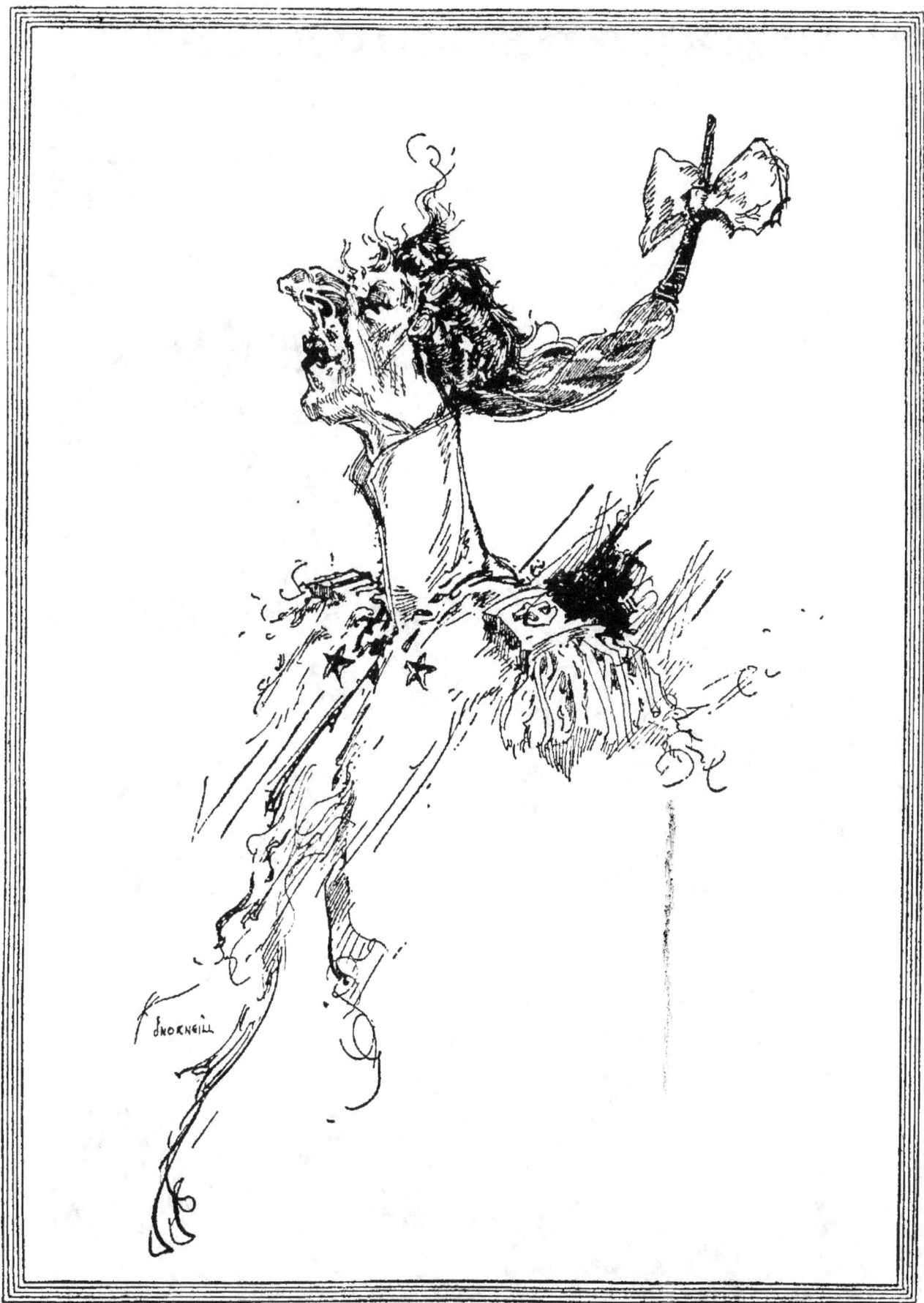

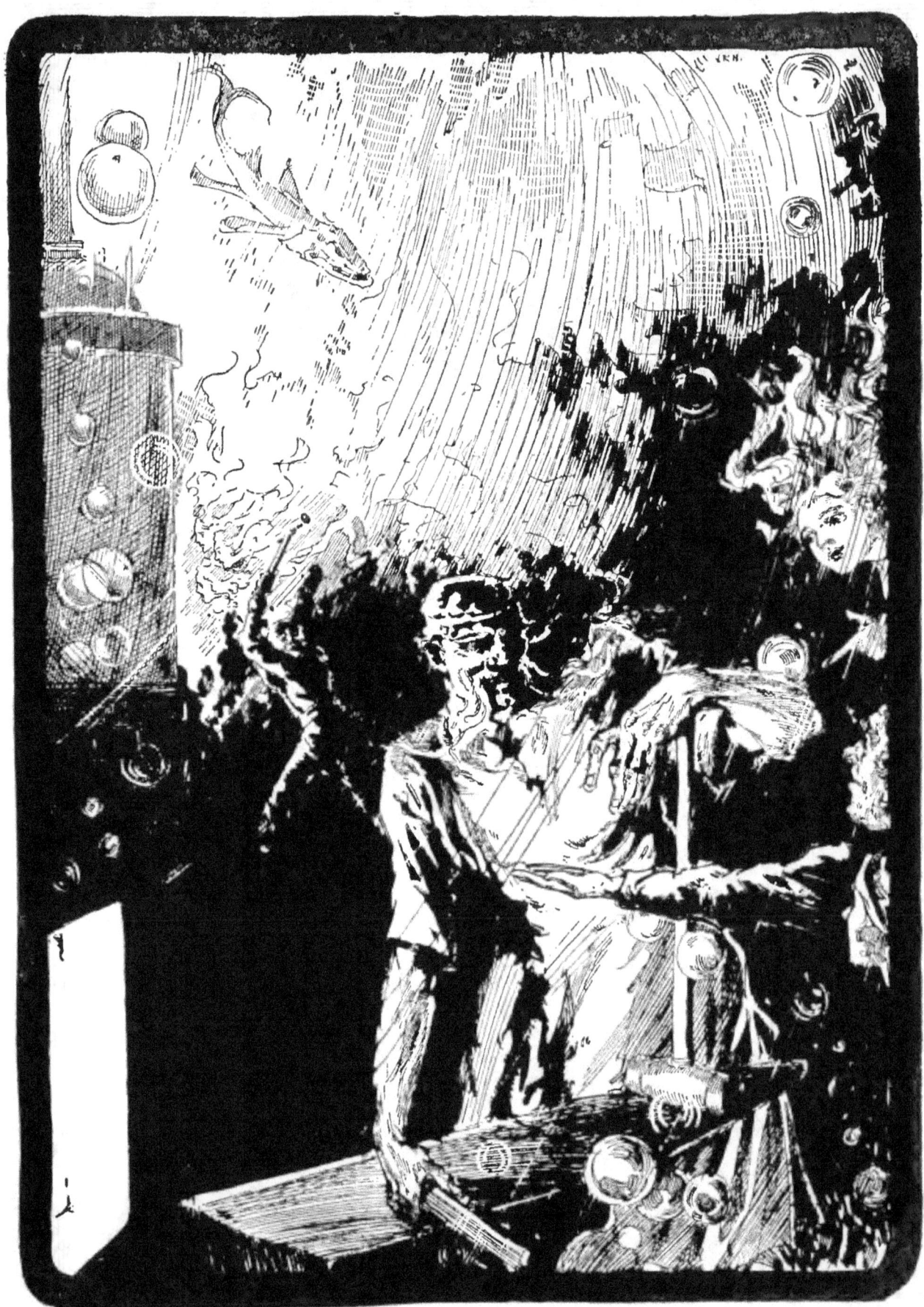

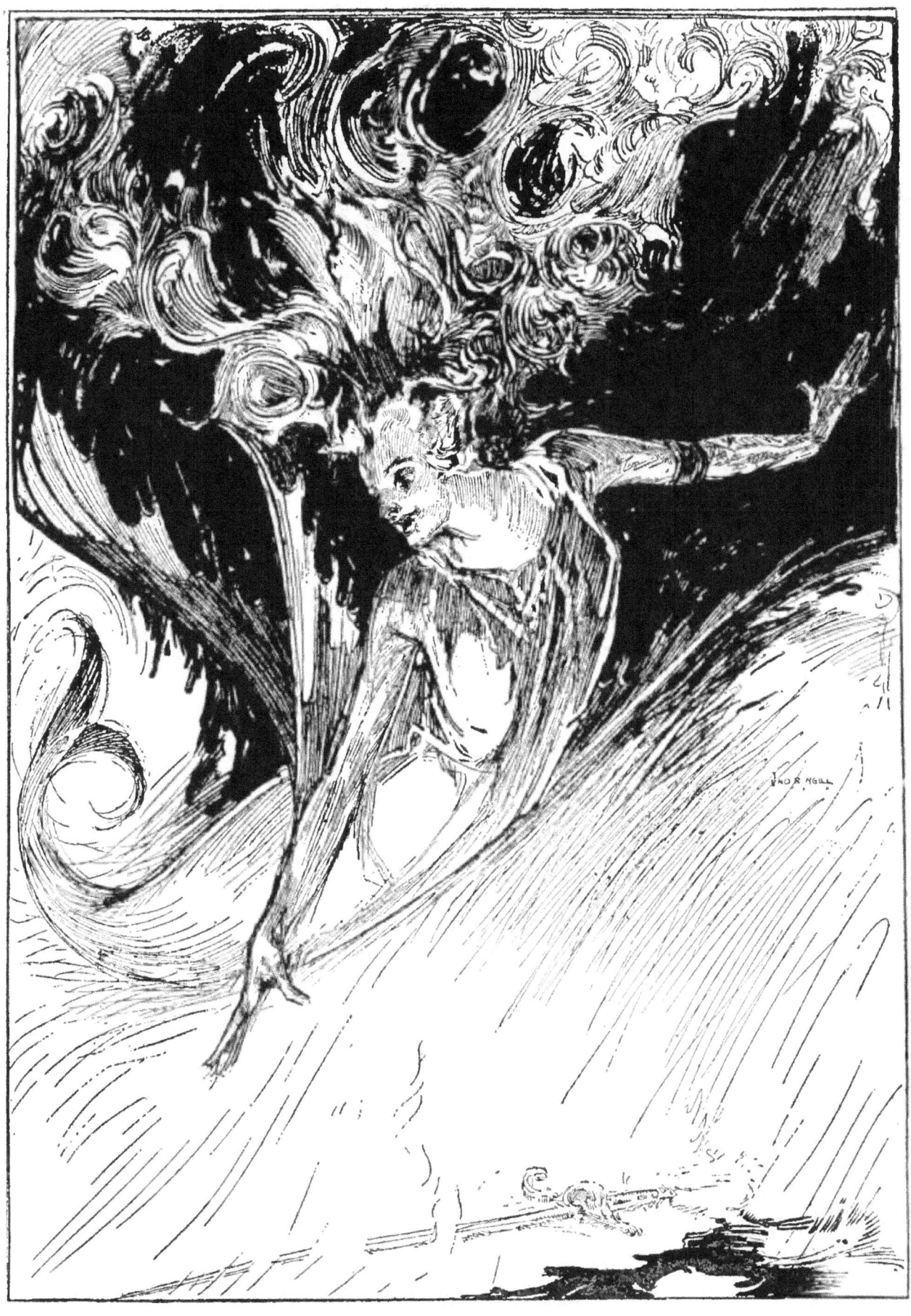

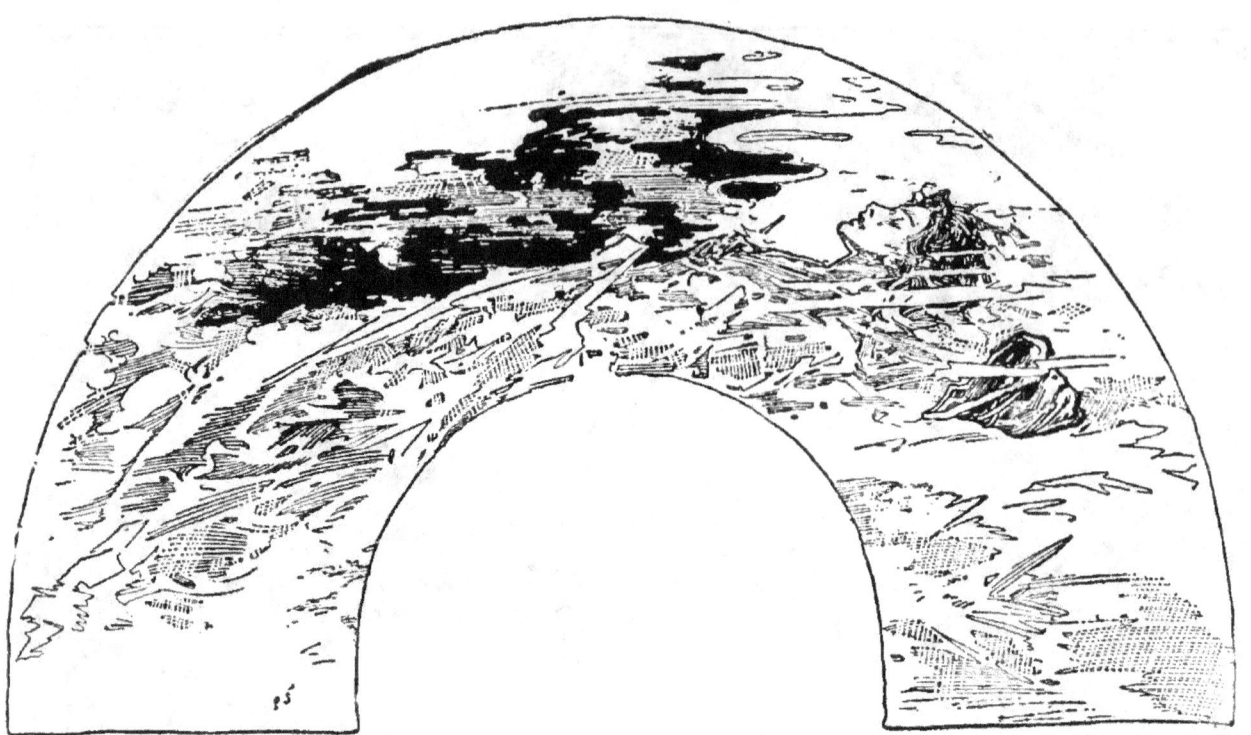

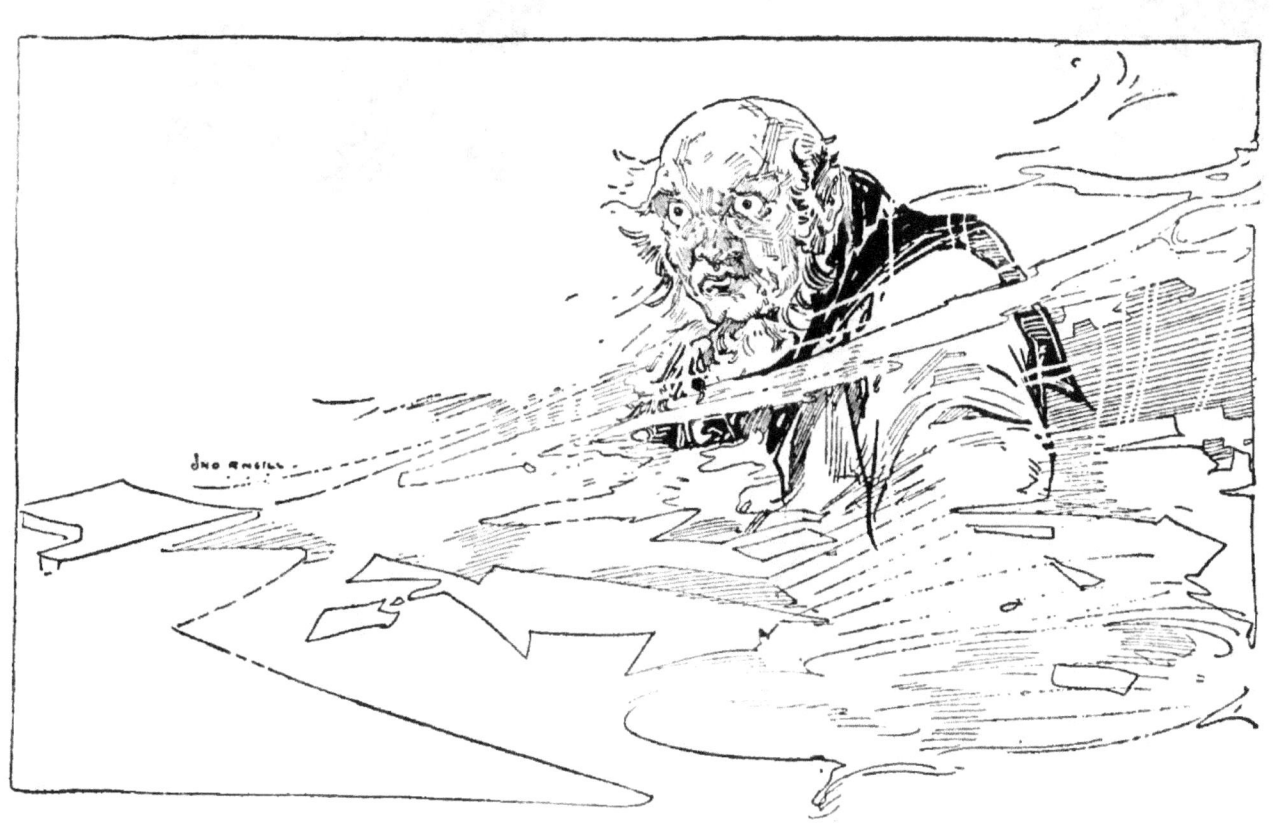

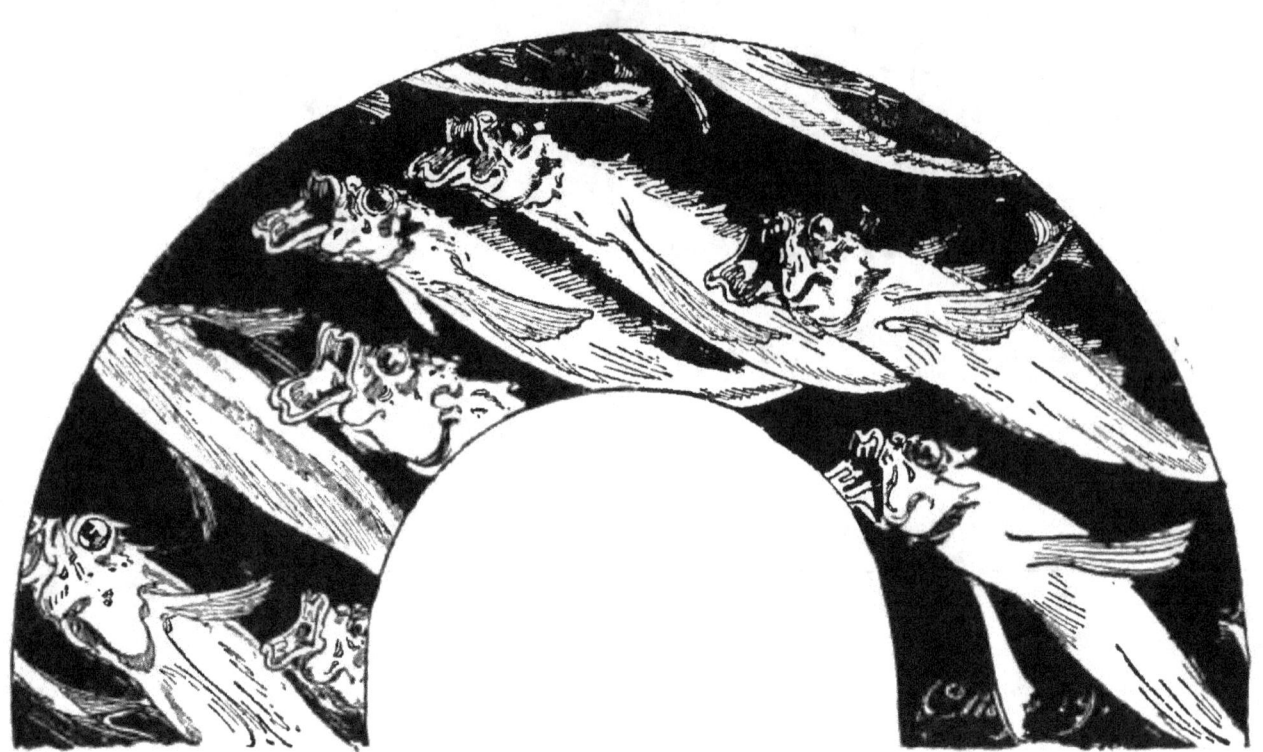

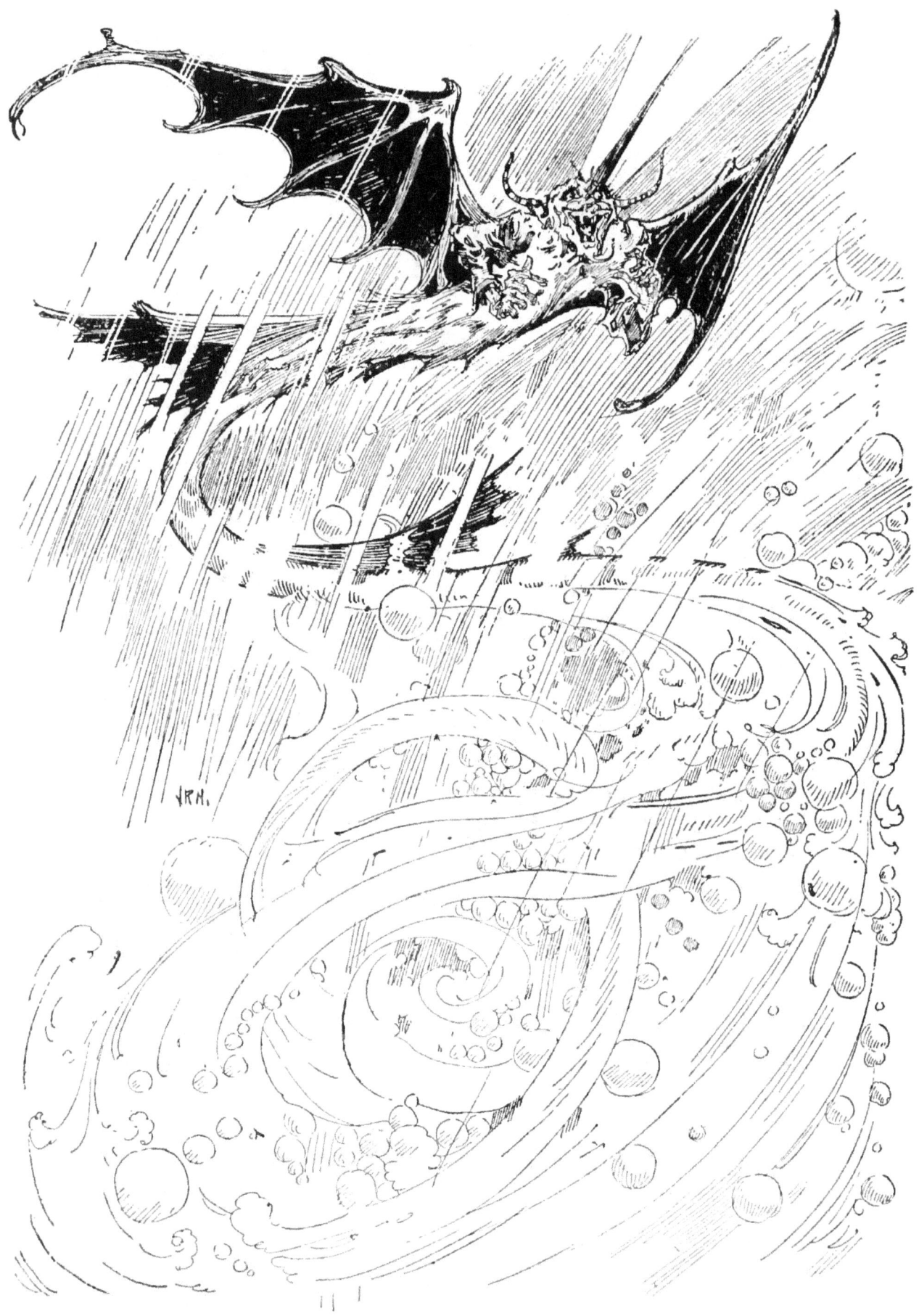

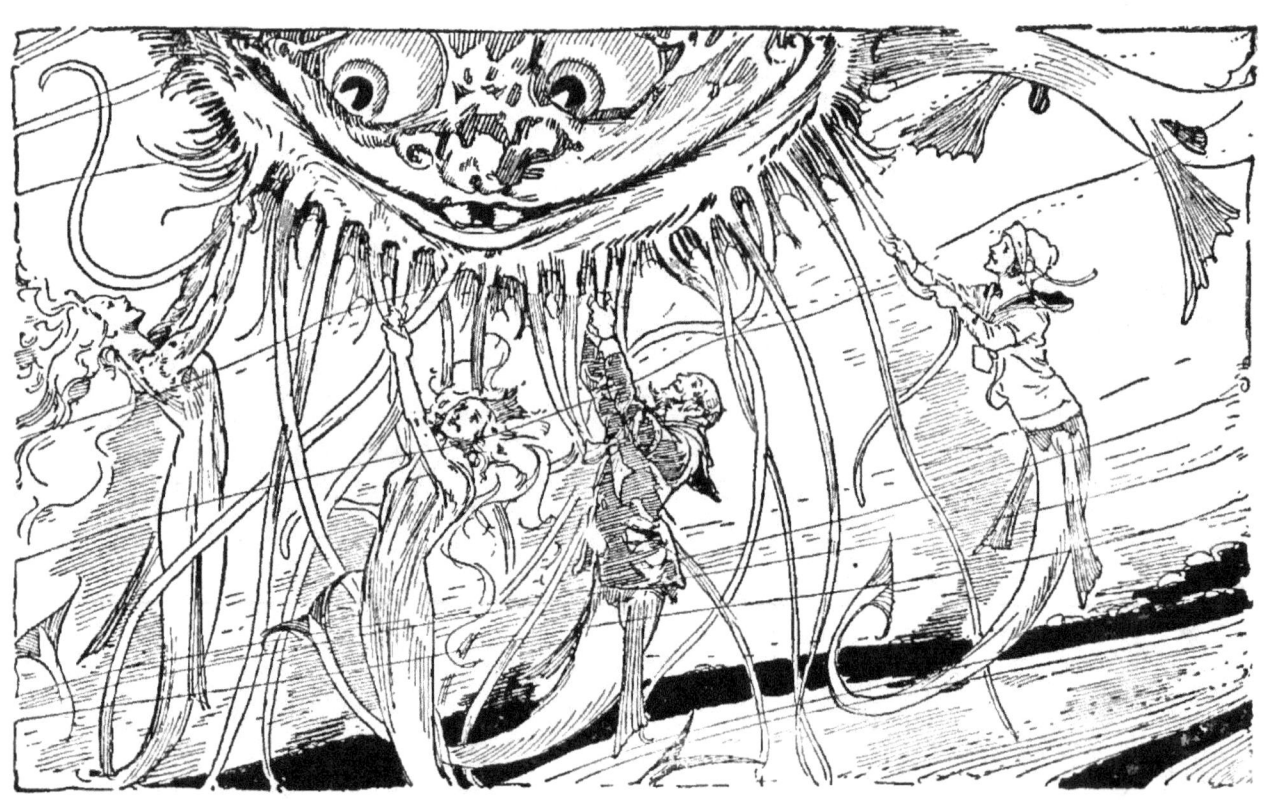

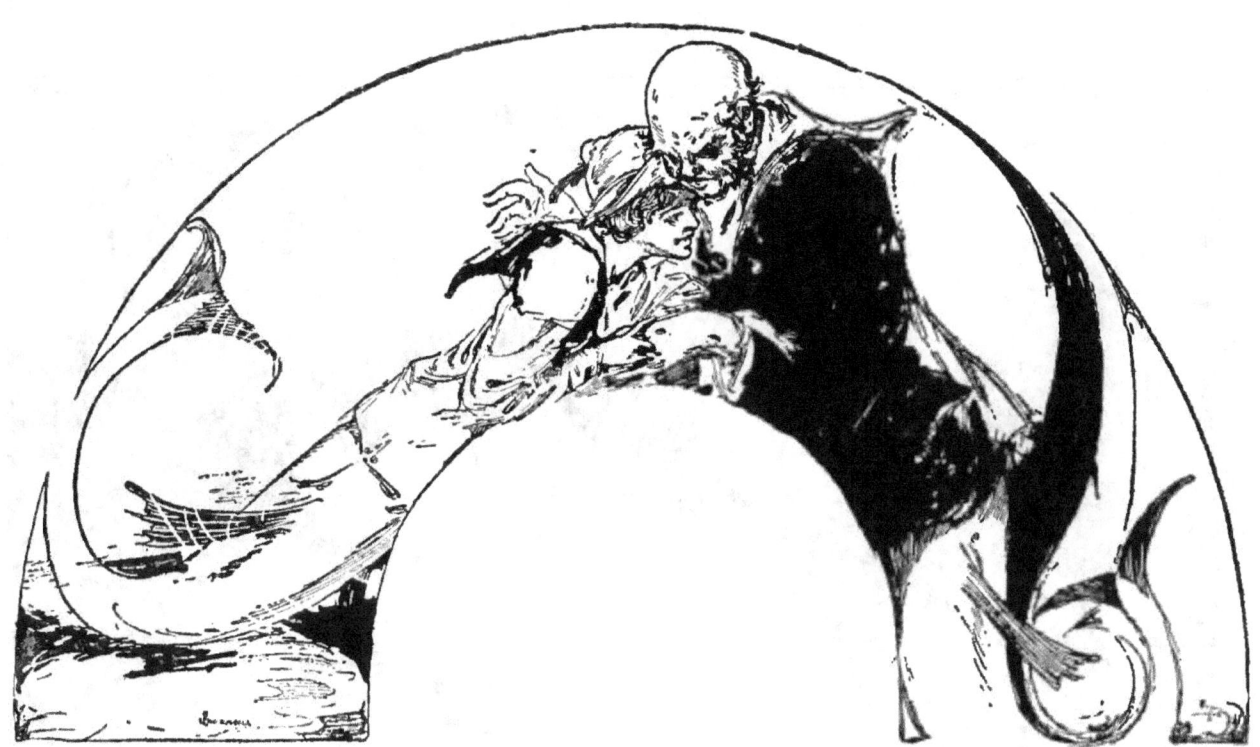

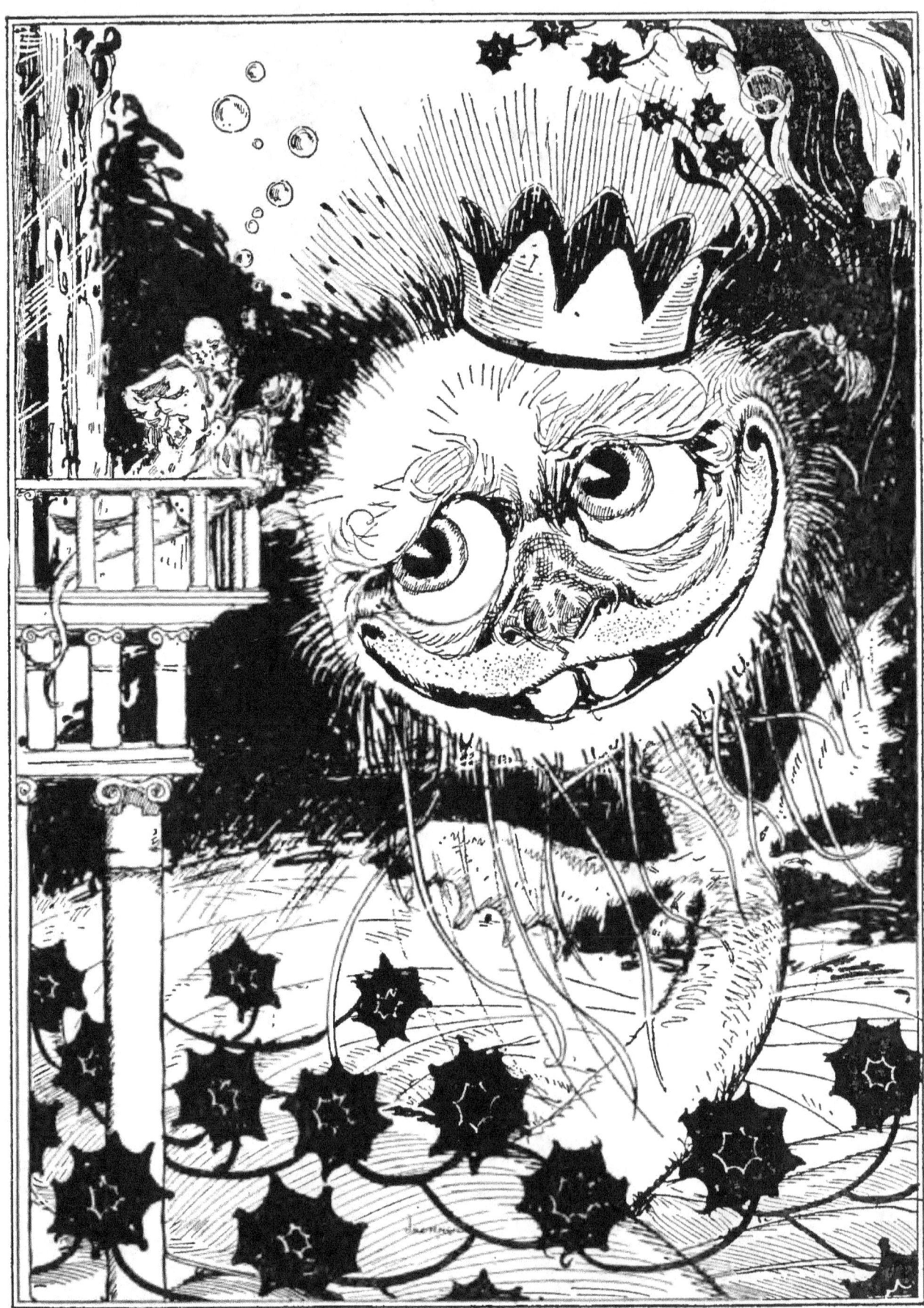

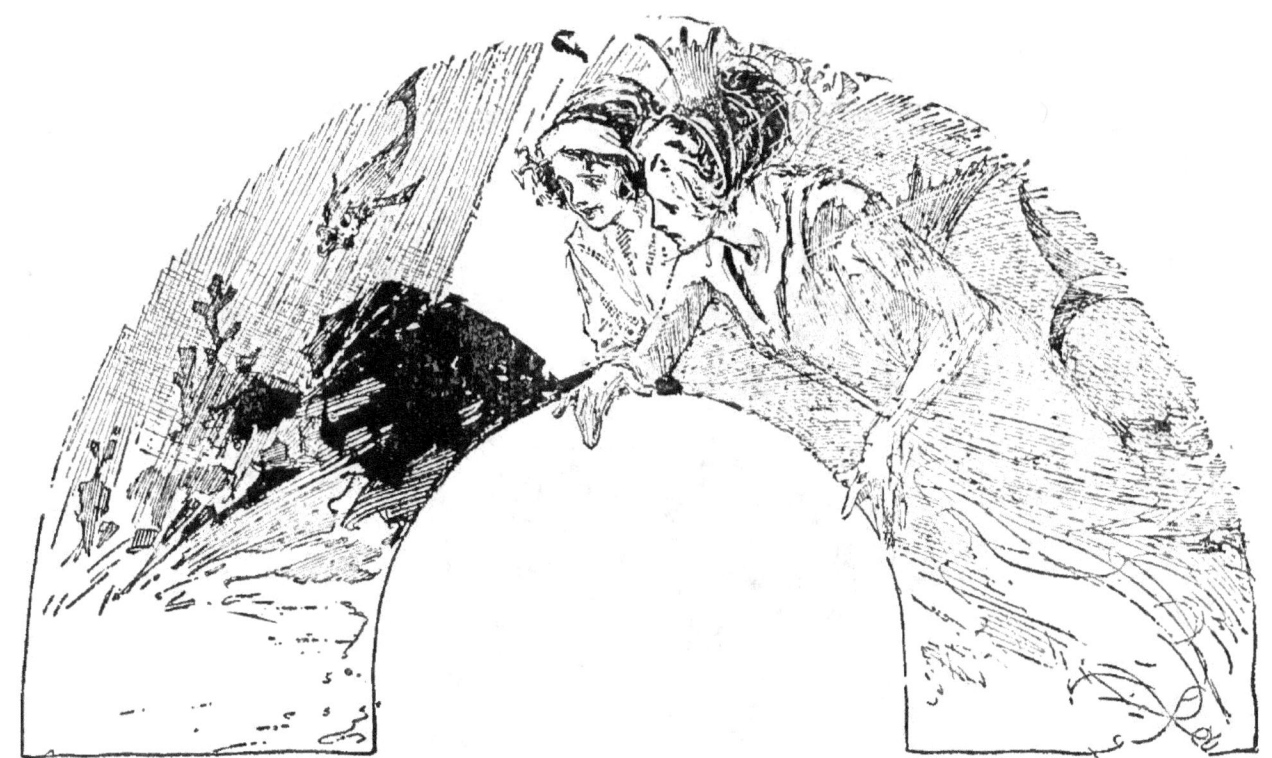

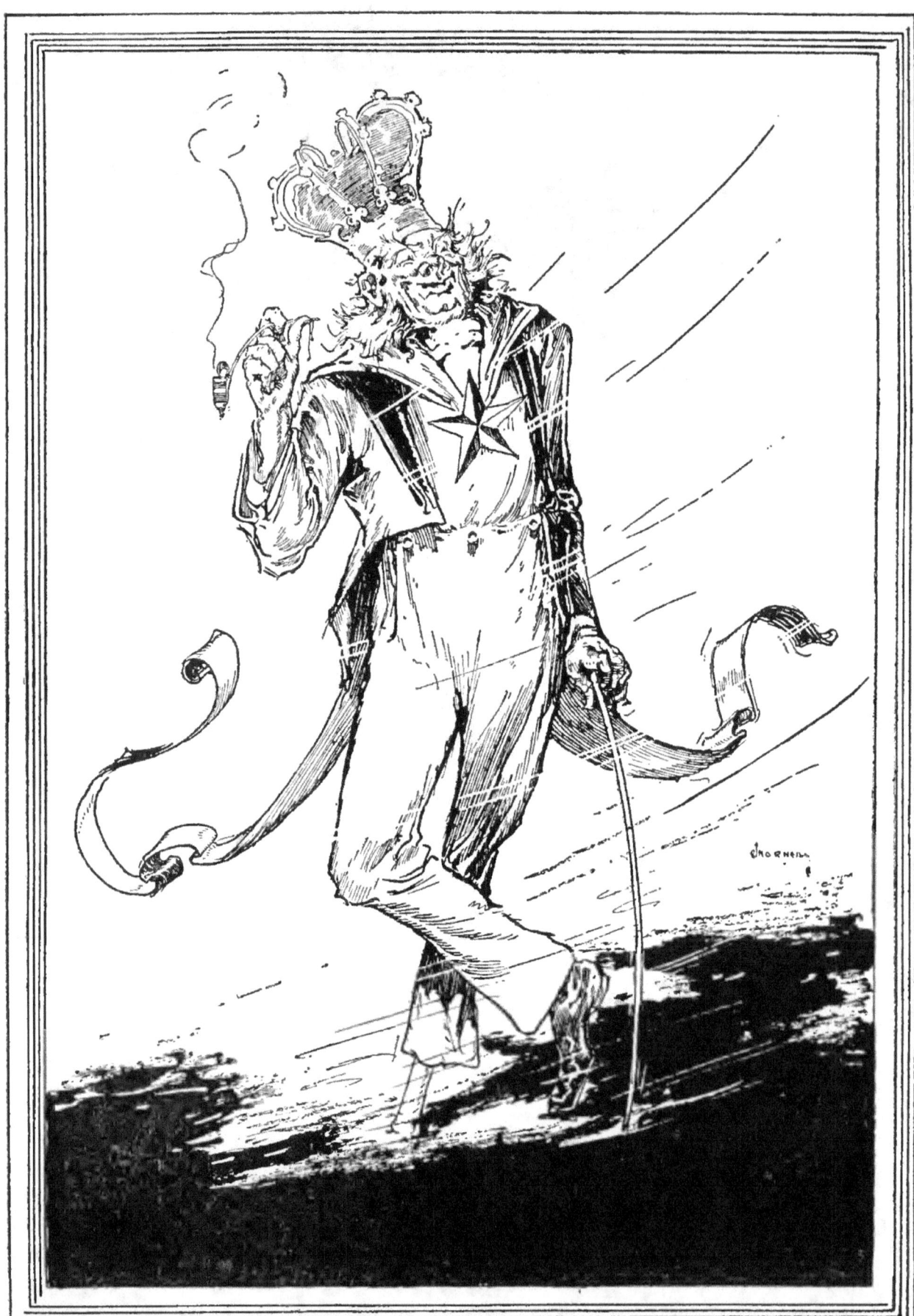

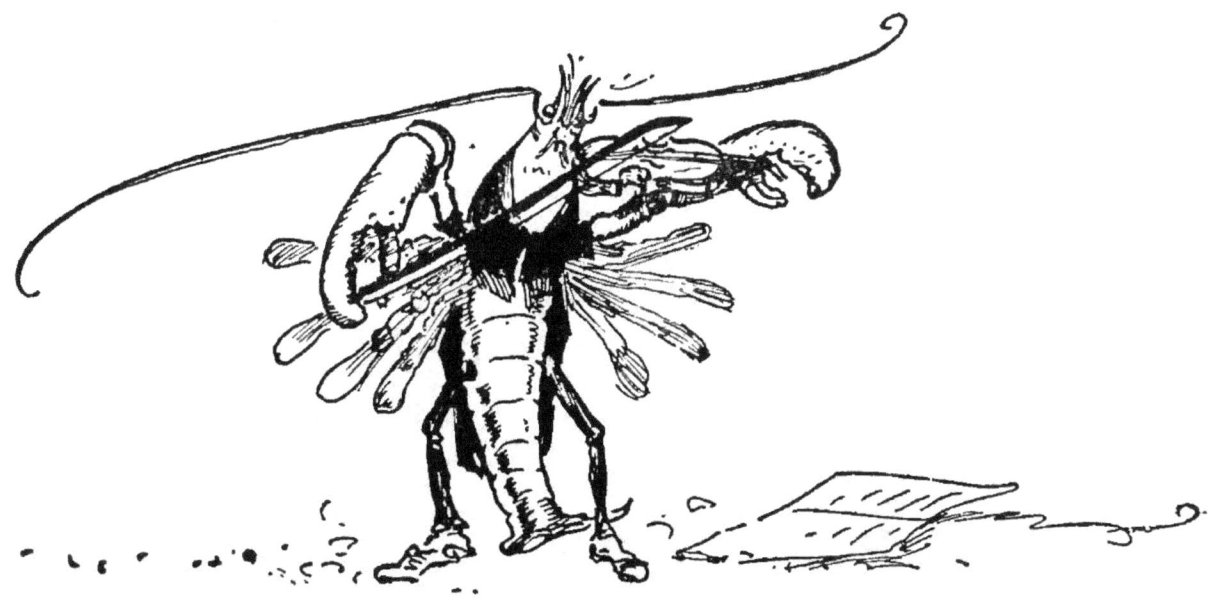

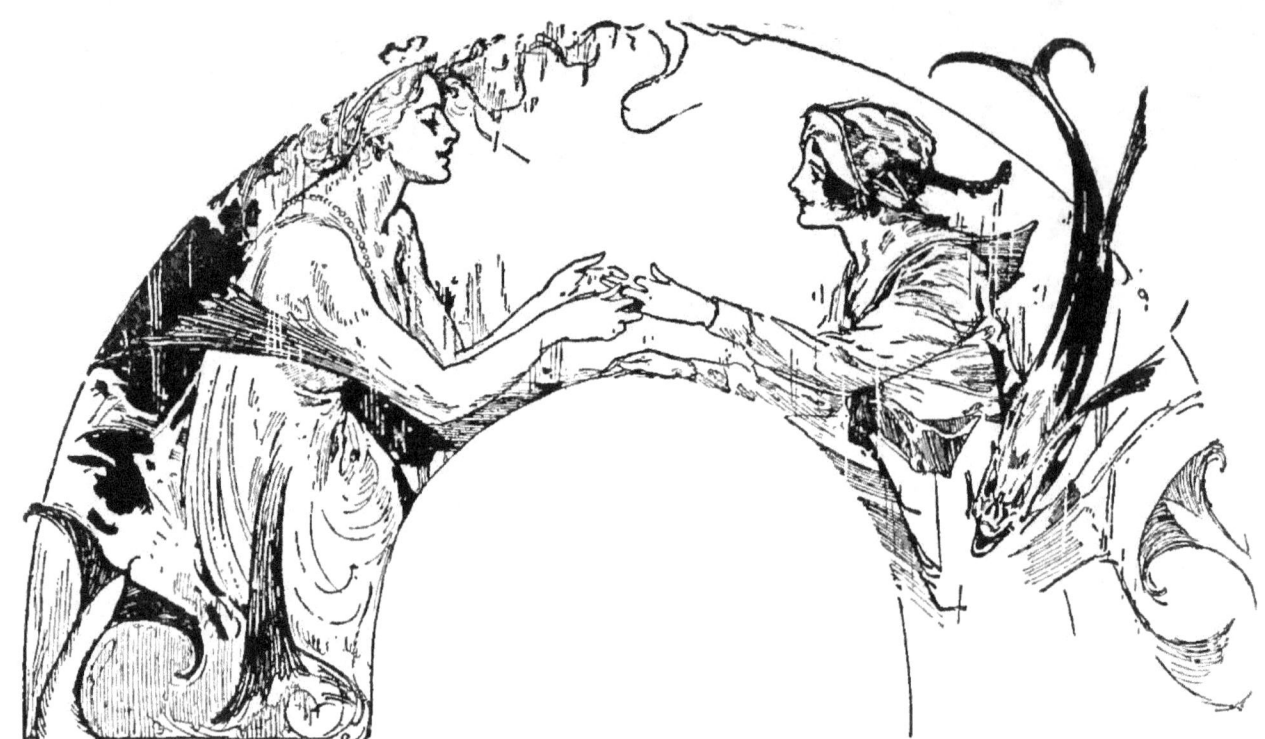

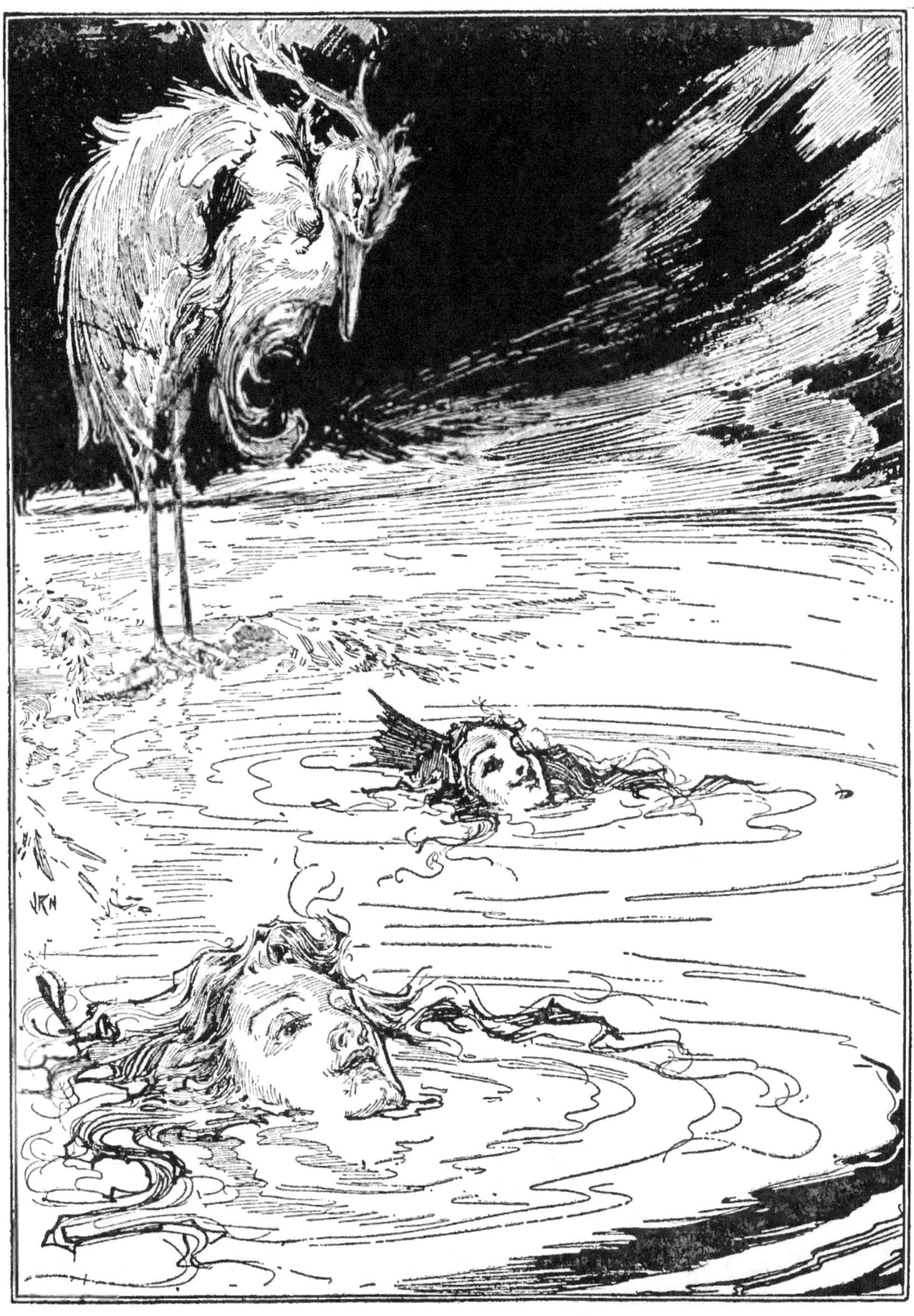

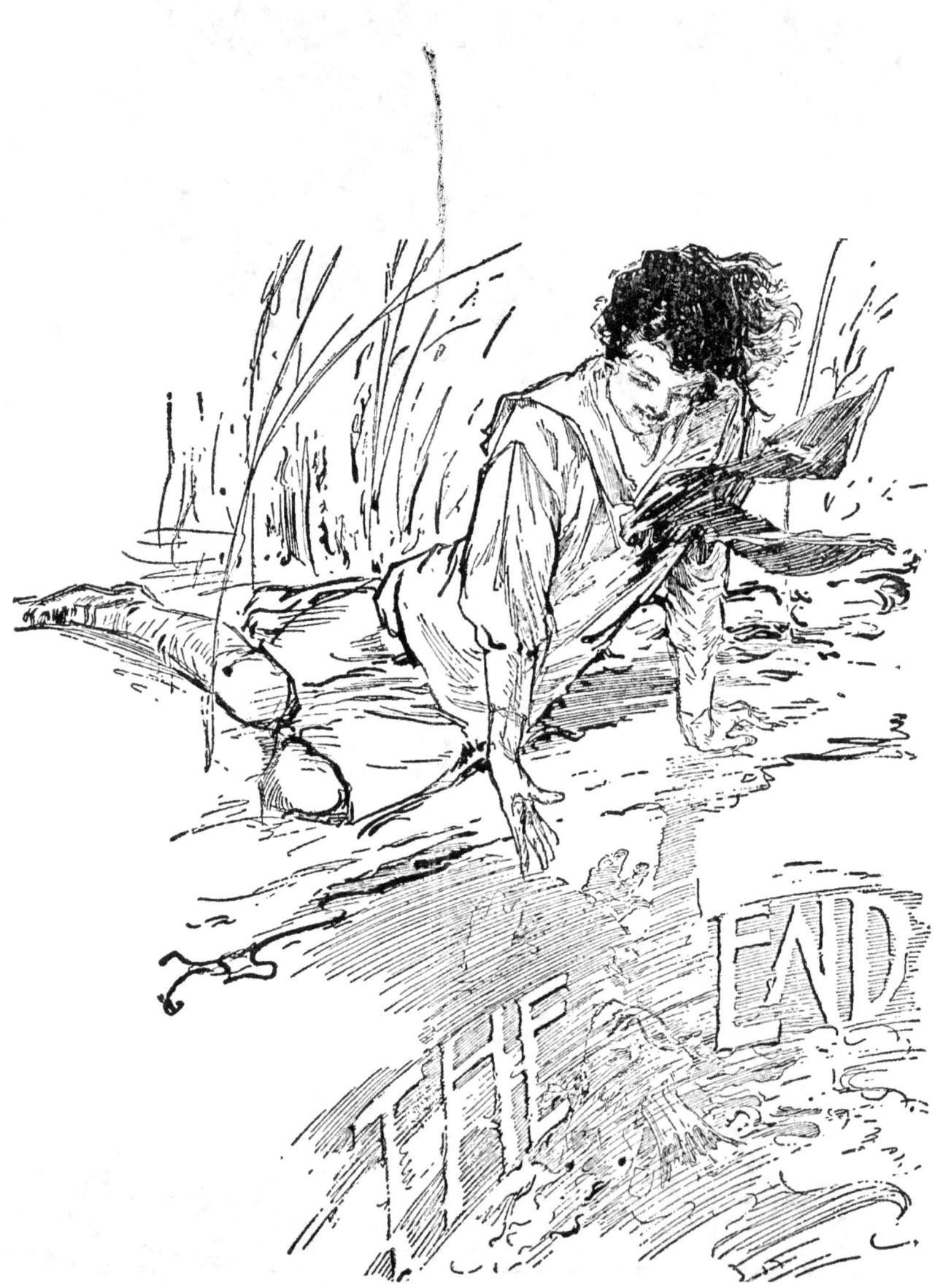

THE END

www.ingramcontent.com/pod-product-compliance
Lightning Source LLC
Chambersburg PA
CBHW081120180526
45170CB00008B/2936